DUPLICATE THIS!

SHOWING YOUR FRIENDS HOW TO LIVE LIKE JESUS

ANDY BRANER ////

 ZONDERVAN®

ZONDERVAN.com/
AUTHORTRACKER
follow your favorite authors

 invert

 youth specialties

youth specialties

Duplicate This!: Showing Your Friends How to Live Like Jesus
Copyright 2008 by Andy Braner

Youth Specialties products, 300 S. Pierce St., El Cajon, CA 92020 are published by Zondervan, 5300 Patterson Ave. SE, Grand Rapids, MI 49530.

Library of Congress Cataloging-in-Publication Data

Braner, Andy.
  Duplicate this! : showing your friends how to live like Jesus / Andy Braner.
    p. cm.
  ISBN-10: 0-310-27754-X (pbk.)
  ISBN-13: 978-0-310-27754-5 (pbk.)
  1. Discipling (Christianity)—Juvenile literature. 2. Evangelistic work—Juvenile literature. 3. Spiritual formation—Juvenile literature. 4. Christian teenagers—Religious life—Juvenile literature. I. Title.
  BV4520.B635 2008
  248'.5—dc22

                                                                    2007041813

All Scripture quotations, unless otherwise indicated, are taken from the *Holy Bible, Today's New International Version*™. TNIV®. Copyright 2001, 2005 by International Bible Society. Used by permission of Zondervan. All rights reserved.

Cover design by Gearbox
Interior design by Mark Novelli

Printed in the United States of America

---

08 09 10 11 12 • 20 19 18 17 16 15 14 13 12 11 10 9 8 7 6 5 4 3 2 1

CONTENTS

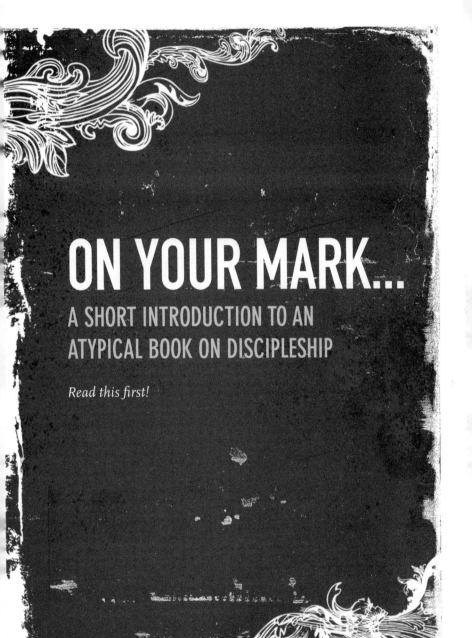

ON YOUR MARK...

A SHORT INTRODUCTION TO AN ATYPICAL BOOK ON DISCIPLESHIP

Read this first!

y previous book, *Love This!*, asked teenagers to re-think their ways of looking at Jesus by seeing that one of the biggest things he stood for was intro-ducing people to practical ways they could love those around them. In fact Matthew 22 reiterates the urgency of Jesus' calling: "Love your neighbor as yourself."

Now teenagers are doing just that: Redefining what it means to have a neighbor and love a neighbor. There are literally thousands of students reaching out to the homeless, helpless, and hopeless of their communities. A revolution is beginning.

So I thought it important to write about another one of Jesus' commands and how teenagers could put it into practice. Matthew 28:19-20 says, "Go therefore and make disciples of all nations, baptizing them in the name of the Father and of the Son and of the Holy Spirit, teaching them to observe all that I have com-manded you. And behold, I am with you always, to the end of the age."

Disciple? What does that mean? Go and make dis-ciples?

Traditional discipleship typically tends to resemble a sort of follow-up program. Kind of like a "training" session for new Christians—all those who've decided to come to the altar and pray to Jesus to come into their hearts. You see, our church culture tends to place disci-pleship after another big word in Christian theology—*evangelism*. In other words, after a person is *evangelized* and becomes a Christian, that person is then *discipled* and trained the ways of the faith. Like I said—a sort of step-by-step method of coming to understand the influence of Jesus in a personal way.

But what if we missed it? What if discipleship means more than "the next step"? It surely doesn't seem that way from Jesus' teaching—that we need to accept him in our hearts first, *then* undergo a radical teaching time to understand more. The *understanding more about Jesus* and the *coming to Jesus* "parts" seemed to happen together with most folks.

So why should we be any different?

Maybe another way to talk about discipleship is to use a word like *duplicate*. That seems to capture the essence of it. After all, isn't the main goal to go out there and help other people understand the love and grace given to you from God? To recreate in others' lives all the amazing things that have happened in your life?

To duplicate.

To make like an original.

To recreate oneself.

To share.

To discuss.

To explore.

To understand.

If I were to boil this book down to a main theme, it would be to reinterpret Jesus' command to make disciples from a "Welcome to the club" approach to a "Hey! Who here wants to know about the greatest message on earth?" perspective. *Duplicate This!* attempts to do just that.

Of course this book works if you're looking to duplicate what you already know (and live) about your faith with another Christian—but you're not limited by that parameter, either. This book is also about evangelism *coupled* with discipleship. You can duplicate your faith with Muslims, Jewish people, Buddhists—people of any faith you choose. Or people of no faith at all. The point is that everyone should have the opportunity to know about Jesus and the life-giving message he preached and accept him and follow him. And it's up to you to take an active role in this process with those around you.

NOT A DEVOTIONAL, BUT A DISCUSSION

This book started off as a devotional—a book in which you might find answers to your spiritual questions. But well into the process I discovered that you don't need any more of those kinds of books. Instead what we need is a big, wide-ranging discussion. A book that becomes a place where students of any level of faith (or no faith at all) can ask each other the hard questions and explore the challenging answers.

See, you won't find "A+ B = C" Christianity in *Duplicate This!* Coming to faith and growing in the faith is way more involved than repeating a simple prayer and meeting with other believers once a week. That's why *Duplicate This!* explores the ins and outs of having heart-provoking, mind-changing conversations that lead not only to faith in Jesus but also to growth in your existing faith.

Nothing is taboo. No stone is unturned. *Duplicate This!* is a place where you're welcome to ask questions, disagree, and discover.

Don't be intimidated by the material. It really isn't rocket science. Some things you'll agree with wholeheartedly; others will send a resounding "Did he really write that down on paper?" feeling through your whole body.

And believe it or not, I hope you experience more of the second feeling. Because when you're exposed to ideas that challenge your faith and drive you to explore it in deeper and deeper ways, that's when true growth happens. When your faith really becomes your own. So I hope some of the ideas in this book challenge the status quo! It's about time we begin using more of the brains God gave us and diligently hammer out the validity of this "Christianity thing." We must ask:

Why do we Christians do what we do?

Why do we Christians believe what we do?

Is there a way for Christian teenagers to succeed in their spiritual journeys?

I think you can!

BUT NOT ON YOUR OWN

The best way to use this book is to invite someone you respect to join you on your journey. It matters not what this person believes—in fact, how exciting would it be to walk through these pages with a person whose spiritual views and understandings are the exact opposite of yours? And then, to top it off, this person begins to understand the depth of the Christian faith while you grow in yours!

And who knows what the Holy Spirit may do?

Much like *Love This!*, *Duplicate This!* is a real-life/real-action type of book. It isn't meant for a quiet reading by the fire 'til you get a warm, fuzzy feeling in your spirit. *Duplicate This!* is intended for movement.

Besides, I don't think Jesus meant for us to sit around with warm, fuzzy feelings all the time anyway. Instead I believe he truly wants us—this specific generation—to usher in a whole new perspective on life.

And guess what? You can do it!

You can challenge your friends to stop living the way they're living and choose revolutionary existences instead. You can model what it might look like to truly care about others. And instead of scrapping for position and harboring jealousy, you can model what it means to encourage and truly love others.

So once again—if you're looking for answers, this isn't the place. If you're looking for a journey, a compass, and a direction sign, *Duplicate This!* is right up your alley. I hope you enjoy this book! I wrote it from the bottom of my soul, and my prayer is that it actually motivates you and other teenagers into movement toward Jesus.

God bless you on your journey!

On my own journey,

Andy Braner

DUPLICATION FOUNDATIONS

The chapters in this section deal with core principles and ideas behind discipleship. *Read this next!*

CHAPTER ONE

IMITATING TRUTH

Brothers, join in imitating me, and keep your
eyes on those who walk according to the
example you have in us. For many, of whom
I have often told you and now tell you even
with tears, walk as enemies of the cross of
Christ. Their end is destruction, their god is
their belly, and they glory in their shame,
with minds set on earthly things. But our
citizenship is in heaven, and from it we
await a Savior, the Lord Jesus Christ, who
will transform our lowly body to be like his
glorious body, by the power that enables him
even to subject all things to himself.

—PHILIPPIANS 3:17-21 (ESV)

Have you ever wanted to play around and pretend you're someone else? Come on—how cool would it be to have some sort of special power, or be someone great in history, or maybe just have a different personality so you could be someone else, even for just a little while. Well, guess what? You can. Courtesy of one of the greatest forms of communication in our world—acting.

Whether on stage or on the big screen, actors have captured our attention and imagination since time began. After all, acting is one of the most effective ways to share experiences, challenge critical thinking, or purely entertain an audience. These days, although many movies aren't worth watching due to their questionable content, every now and then you find a great one, maybe even a classic—such as *City Slickers*.

It's not that it's an epic work of art; the magic of *City Slickers* is all about the group of actors collaborating to tell the story of a middle-aged man navigating mortality.

Mitch Robbins is an advertising salesman, played by Billy Crystal, who falls into a serious depression on the evening of his 40th birthday. In order to help him out of it, his friends take him on an adrenaline-filled cattle drive in the most beautiful parts of the western U.S.

Mitch and his friends are completely unprepared. Instead of the sound of honking horns in the streets, these city slickers are forced to live with the moan of the cattle in the pen, use old-fashioned outhouses, and survive without creature comforts and familiar things. Instead of dodging pedestrians in crosswalks, they're dodging the pain of horseback riding day in, day out.

The trail boss, Curly, is a 70-year-old man, wrinkled from years in the sun. The kind of guy who shaves with a bowie knife; who carries an air of intimidation everywhere he goes. When Curly enters the scene, a strange music whistles in the background to warn the audience of his presence. A cast of cowboys add further ambiance to the recreation of a real cattle drive.

The *City Slickers* writers did an incredible job of integrating humor. I mean I love to laugh, but sometimes I find it hard to laugh out loud in the theater. This movie had me laughing uncontrollably. My side hurt so badly sometimes I couldn't breathe.

It was a great film, but none of it would have been possible if the actors didn't sell their characters. They understood that the various nuances of each character added to the overall feel of the story. The actors used their abilities to become different people, and the sum of their efforts helped create a cinematic classic.

After I saw *City Slickers*, I decided this craft of acting was something I had to do. A calling? An intuition? Maybe just the possibility that I could be good at something? I don't know what the draw was, but one thing I knew for certain—it was extremely important for me to create. I had to be involved in an art form that communicated big ideas to an audience.

Biology was too structured.

English had too many grammatical lessons.

Engineering? Yeah, right. I haven't been good at math since the day the maternity doctor slapped me on the behind and said, "Welcome to the world!"

I felt it in my gut—I had to become an actor; I had to create in this way. I was compelled to indulge my life in the stories of different characters to ultimately make a difference in the world. I figured if I could logically present an idea onstage, I might be able to address social problems plaguing the human condition.

As I think back now, it seems pretty clear. God chiseled in me a desire to tell stories, but to that point in my life, the only storytelling I'd been doing was when I was trying to act cool in front of girls at the freshman dance. The year I saw *City Slickers*, girls were the most important part of life, but something deep inside kept calling, *There has to be something more than this dating scene.*

The theater directed my energy in positive, productive ways. I was determined to master characters and collaborate with others to bring about true forms of stories that we could use to develop a laboratory of thinking. It wasn't that I wanted to be in the spotlight; I simply desired to help people think about certain issues by using my newfound artistic medium.

And so, acting became my life. I threw everything I had into mastering the craft. Everything I read was theater. Every job I took was strategically designed to grow my imagination. I watched people eat. I watched people talk. I watched people walk. I went to school and rehearsed for hours on end, and I can truly say it became my obsession.

Think of the great plays you've been exposed to: *Hamlet, Julius Caesar, Romeo and Juliet*—all masterpieces. But they aren't good stage productions without good actors. When *Hamlet* is performed well, you don't even notice the difficult language, and the story leaps from the stage. In fact, for a split second you can feel that strange emotion inside your soul compelling you to understand truth.

You want to kill the king.

You feel betrayed by your mother.

You want to rise to the throne and make all things right.

You feel the ghost of your father whispering to you in the night.

Hamlet ceases to exist, and you become the Danish prince.

That's why I wanted to be an actor.

I wanted to harness the artistic part of my life and create a moving piece of work that forced an audience to look at the core of its collective existence and ask, "Why?"

It didn't matter if my vehicle was *City Slickers* or *Hamlet*; I was dedicated to posing certain questions to a populace so it could see life from a different angle. I wanted audiences to ask questions such as...

Why do I live like I do?

Why do I act like I do?

Do I really believe what I say?

How would I respond in that situation?

All are questions well worth the price of an admission ticket; and more than merely playing characters, I wanted to propose problems that could lead others to find solutions.

Sure, you can look at a painting and be moved, but what if the painting could talk? What if the painting could sing? What if the painting could give you various options for belief? That's what good actors do, and to be good, you have to learn a few tricks of the trade. You have to create a palette of invisible colors so that a piece can come alive.

IMITATION (ACTING 101)

My first lesson in acting was a bit of an awkward situation. I decided if I wanted to learn, I'd best begin taking a class. So I showed up for the first day and thought, "This is the greatest decision of my life."

The professor emphasized the fact that every actor must learn how to imitate. Much like a painter at her first easel, the prof told us it takes a bit of copying to learn how to create certain strokes and color combinations so an audience can find an actor believable: "You have to forget who you are and imitate the character you're trying to be."

He held up flashcards of various people, animals, or emotions, and we had to imitate the cards to create believable scenes. The animals seemed like a sure bet; some of the others seemed as though they'd pose a challenge.

One card had a picture of an elephant and another, a dog. But try acting like the Empire State Building, and acting might quickly become one of the hardest things you've ever done.

Our class didn't have a script. We didn't have any direction. Just simple imitation. Sounds easy, right? Well, it wasn't so simple. Pour everything you know about an object into a 45-minute evolution of character, try and cease to be you and become something else. That's where actors split. Anybody can dance around stage and try to be something—we do that every time we play charades; but try to make someone believe you *are* the charade—that's acting.

Well, as you might imagine, I got stuck with one of the most difficult cards.

I tried to peek at some of my friends' cards so I could prepare for the ensuing challenge. The first one was a car. "Come on—how easy is that?" *Vroom vroom.* The sound of the engine would be a dead giveaway.

The next one was Julia Roberts. *Okay,* I thought, *I might have a problem playing a poor prostitute stuck in the hills of L.A., but most people are familiar enough with* Pretty Woman *that it shouldn't be so difficult.*

My first card? A duck.

That's right, you read it correctly. A duck.

So for the next 45 minutes, not only did I have to figure out how to convince my classmates that I was sane (which, by the way, is tough when you're quacking around the room), but I also had to bring them into a willing suspension of disbelief. I had to become a duck.

The teacher asked if there were any questions and then released the class to go anywhere in this black room and figure out how to be whatever the picture on the card demanded.

I slipped into the corner and thought, *There's no way. How in the world am I going to change from being a 200-pound guy to a five-pound duck?* But determined to learn the tricks of the acting trade, I started quacking around the room. (I'm sure glad YouTube wasn't around then.)

I squatted down on my ankles and held my arms to the side as if I had duck wings. I began the traditional *quack quack* noise ducks make, but something wasn't right. I didn't sound much like a real duck. I sounded like a two-year-old learning about ducks for the first time.

My professor confronted me: "Andy, come on. You've got to imagine you're a duck. You've got to become a duck. Think about what a duck looks like. Think about what he really talks like. Think about other duck characters you've seen. Believe you are a DUCK!"

I was totally confused, "But I'm not a du..."

"It's ACTING, BRANER!"

Frustrated to no end, I remembered Donald Duck. (You know, from old-school Disney? Mickey Mouse's buddy?) He walks around quacking his speech, and audiences barely understand what he's saying. Maybe if I tried to imitate Donald, I could create my own duck-like language. It was totally unintelligible, but I thought if Donald could talk to Mickey, and Mickey could always understand him, then surely this couldn't be that difficult.

So, I started wobbling around the room, trying to remember how Donald talked. It came out a little weird at first, but as I kept on going and going, it was as if I really started becoming the duck. It wasn't like I was growing wings and a bill or anything, but I started imitating a duck. With a little makeup and a few feathers, I very well might have pulled off a convincing performance.

"There you go. Keep going. What does the duck want? What does the duck eat? Where is the duck wobbling?" My teacher commanded over the class. (I'm convinced that if a video of that performance ever got out, the world would know I'm crazy!)

I was low to the ground. I was making Donald Duck sounds. And before long, my body actually started swaying from side to side. I was in the process of convincing my class that I was no longer Andy, but I was really evolving into a duck.

I know. You're probably thinking, *Man, if they teach that class when I go to college, I'm taking it!* But don't be fooled. It takes a lot of work to truly imitate something as seemingly simple as a duck—and persuade an audience to believe it. Great actors have to know how their characters will walk, how they'll talk, and how they'll respond to any situation, and I wanted to learn how to become a great actor.

I watched the greats. I saw *Last of the Mohicans* and witnessed Daniel Day-Lewis imitate the life of a Native American. At first I thought he actually had some sort of Native background, but that wasn't the case. To prepare for the role, he lived on a North American Indian reservation. He worked right alongside the Native Americans making stuff, wearing moccasins, and learning firsthand the culture he was about to represent. True to the details of his craft, Lewis made his character one of the most believable in all of movie history.

Johnny Depp does the same as Captain Jack Sparrow in *Pirates of the Caribbean*. If you notice, he walks totally differently from any other character he's ever played. He uses a unique speech pattern. The costume choice forces his body to move a certain way. His eyes dart around like I imagine a crazy pirate's eyes would move.

Some actors call it a *method*, meaning there's a method to becoming someone else. You have to think like he thinks. You have to walk like she walks. You have to talk like he talks. And if done right, your performance will convince the audience that you're actually the person you're trying to imitate. It's an amazing craft, and when I was a freshman in college, I started imitating all sorts of people.

I took various jobs at college so I could study people's quirks. I became an EMT so I could ride in an ambulance and expose myself to more and more human nuances. I worked at a tuxedo store in the mall hemming pants, just so I could pick up the smallest details and use them in my next creation. I took this acting thing WAY seriously. Nobody was going to stop me from becoming what I wanted to become.

IMITATION IN LIFE

Imitating isn't only an acting trick. We imitate others all the time. We dress like people we think are cool looking. We talk like high-profile people in our culture. Even our hairstyles are imitations, chosen to get others to think we're like somebody famous.

I was getting my hair cut just the other day and started a conversation with a stylist. "Do people really bring in magazines to imitate hairstyles of the rich and famous?" I asked.

"Absolutely," the stylist said. "It's funny, too. They bring those pictures in here so they can look like someone else, and I have to tell them, 'Look, I can cut your hair like it looks in that picture, but I can't make you look like a movie star.'"

We live in a surreal time—marked by our constant drive to imitate people we believe are important.

While that may seem kind of lame, imitation just happens to be an important, beginning step in becoming the people we're supposed to be. A baby imitates sounds made by his mother and father to learn language. A basketball player begins learning how to shoot by imitating other players who're draining three-pointers.

SPIRITUAL IMITATION

Just as we imitate in life, we imitate in our Christian lives. Spiritual imitation is the first part of understanding how Jesus wants us to live. Imitation has been used in the church since its inception, and Christians actually learn how to live life as they pass on their faith through imitation.

When Jesus called his disciples, he said, "Come and follow me"—in other words, "Come and watch what I do and then go out and do the same." Come imitate me. Come do the exact things I do, and I'll show you the meaning of my life.

It's so cool that the God of the universe had a mission to take 12 men and duplicate divine power and love right here on the earth. God was so intentional about transferring it to them that God actually came and lived with them. Isn't that amazing? God came to live with humans and imitate human life, the very life God created, so we could know the right way to live.

Jesus wants you to imitate the things he did while he was here on the planet so the world can know God's love. He isn't interested in waving a magic wand and instantly turning you into a finished work of art. No, he wants you to simply "come and follow"—and he will help you figure out this "Christian life." This imitation is a journey with God, not an immediate arrival to a known destination.

BELIEVING

Once you begin to master the craft of imitating nuances, the next step in method acting is to actually start to believe who you are.

I once had a director for a play called *The Voice of the Prairie*. It was a wholesome, down-home show about the invention of the radio in the early 1900s. The play chronicles the use of radio and the link between the radio and the ease of communication today and then ultimately showed how the television would change communication in another generation.

I was cast as the protagonist, and through the course of imitating a young Midwestern man, I actually began to believe I was that man when I was onstage. No longer content with just "play acting," I was intentionally beginning to believe I was that person for that time so the audience would believe in my performance. I figured if they believed my character, then the story could be told. If I tried to "act" like someone else, I was confident the audience would have smelled the fakery a mile away. It was my first big shot in front of a mainstage crowd.

I believed so the story would hold weight.

I believed so the audience would believe.

Believing is different from imitating. Once you believe, your whole mindset changes. The "you" fades behind the ambiance you create, because to believe is to convince. If an actor is successful at convincing herself that she is who she's playing, then her choices to talk a certain way, move a certain way, or even create certain facial expressions become second nature. The simplest details invade the core of who you are and transform you into the person you will be.

It's a law of human behavior. Once people begin to buy into an idea of who they are, their actions begin to reflect those beliefs. Belief is the beginning of action, and your actions begin to develop the character you present to the world. It's an important piece of your personality, and it calls you to take seriously the question, "What do you believe?"

Jesus says, "Whoever believes in me, believes not in me but in him who sent me. And whoever sees me sees him who sent me. I have come into the world as light, so that whoever believes in me may not remain in darkness" (John 12:44-46, ESV).

If you're going to buy into Christianity, it's essential that you understand the importance of belief. This belief isn't played out on stage—it's real life. Serious stuff. Jesus' light here on earth chases away darkness—because of belief.

Belief heals blindness.

Belief casts out demons.

Belief is the cornerstone of everything we are.

Without belief, it's impossible to live a life worthy of Christ's calling.

BECOMING

The best actors can convince themselves they really are the people they're becoming—at least for a short time. I'm sure that's why most actors take time out from their work between projects.

They become the hero.

They become the criminal.

They become the hopeless romantic.

They become the people they imitate.

Actors have to take time to cross back over the threshold of real life and become themselves again. Otherwise some of them become convinced they can save the world, while others really believe they're mass murderers.

If the story calls for an actor to be a loving husband, he will actually become a loving husband. If the movie calls for a romantic relationship, sometimes an actor finds herself engulfed in the story and actually begins a real-life romance with her opposite character. You don't have to look very hard to watch Hollywood marriages dissolve because of affairs that start on the set.

When you begin to act like someone else, and you actually believe in what you're doing, you will become that person. That's why it's so important that, as a Christian, you're filling your mind with beliefs that are true.

Truth based on evidence.

Truth based on real life.

Truth that can be verified through many reliable sources.

The essence of becoming a true disciple of Jesus is simple: Believe in Jesus and become like Jesus.

IMITATING JESUS

It's easy to write down, but hard to put into practice.

Paul tells all Christians we are baptized in the same Spirit (1 Corinthians 12), and that's true. This book certainly isn't a conversation about conversion from the old you to the new you. This book attempts to answer questions Christian teenagers are asking about their own spiritual journeys.

Every reference to conversion in the Bible speaks of confession, belief, and obedience. In other words, confession isn't the only component. You have to imitate (obedience), believe (belief), and become (confession). It seems discipleship is nothing less than imitating God.

But how can you imitate someone you've never seen?

You have to watch someone imitate Jesus so you can, too.

You have to watch someone mirror the concept of belief so you can, too.

You have to explore the life of someone who has become like Jesus so you can become like Jesus, too.

The road is an individual one accompanied by the deep fellowship of community commonly found among fellow believers. It's a path you can only know inside you, but you must seek help on the outside to enrich the quality of your spiritual life—by listening to real people around you who've walked the road before you.

The sole intent of this book is to invite you to realize those basic fundamental truths, so you can then share them with people in your life.

Become an imitator so others can imitate you.

Become a believer so others can believe, too.

Become a follower of Jesus so others can follow also.

Some of these foundational bricks are easy, and others are widely debated and difficult to reconcile. The Bible says, "But seek first the kingdom of God and his righteousness, and all these things will be added to you" (Matthew 6:33, ESV).

It's in the search where God reveals himself to you.

It's in the discovery where truth will come alive and imitating will begin to lead you to becoming the very person God created you to be.

However, it's not the end of the story. Once you've discovered God's righteousness in all its beauty, it's imperative that you duplicate yourself by sharing what you know with someone else. A friend of mine admitted recently, "You have to get rid of your concept of 'destination' and remember life is a journey on which you interact with others." How profound. Getting rid of my idea of destination frees me to walk this journey every day, because the love of God shouldn't be confined to some unrealistic sense of arrival.

It doesn't mean you walk around the school with a big "mule-sized" Bible, beating others into conversion.

It doesn't mean you have the right to argue someone at work into a "God-only" kind of corner. The concept of duplication happens between two people who desire to know God in their innermost beings.

It's something special; because to transfer God's love from one person to another is as beautiful as watching the stars light up in the heavens.

It's deeper than all the oceans.

It's taller than the highest mountains.

It's richer than the colors of a beautiful painting.

It's more real than a great acting performance.

Jesus makes it a process, and he desires first for you to know the process and then go and share the process with others.

He told his disciples to "come," and then in his final hours on earth, he commanded them to "go."

Come and go.

Those are two of the most important commands in all of Christianity.

Are you ready?

CHAPTER TWO

CUT AND RUN

You gotta know when to hold 'em

Know when to fold 'em

Know when to walk away

Know when to run.

—KENNY ROGERS, "THE GAMBLER"

'm not a fan of gambling. In fact, I've hardly ever even done it—for real, that is. But one thing I know about gamblers: If money is on the line, they know when to cut and run. They know if a table's gone cold and their luck is down, it's time to get out of Dodge. Sure, there's always a casual idiot, and that's how the gaming companies make all their money.

Gaming companies long for the guy who gets down on his luck because they know he'll keep throwing out cash in hopes of hitting the jackpot. That guy might as well take his cash and throw it out of the window of some high-rise. When something is of value to you, you protect it—and discipleship is no different.

Unfortunately, some of us have become the jackpot people in the Christian faith. We continue to sit at the table of discipleship failure and keep on plugging away. I recently read statistics that said in 70 major moral areas, evangelical Christians are no different from non-Christians. We keep on saying we're trying to fulfill the Great Commission, but something's not lining up.

Depression among teenagers is at an all-time high.

Sexual promiscuity is at an all-time high.

Hopelessness is at an all-time high.

Moral choices are continuing to decline in the lives of teenagers around the country.

Summer after summer, I watch Christians come to our summer camp in Colorado for a shot of God in their lives. And we, the church, just keep on steamrolling ahead as if we're going to get it right someday. Not to throw a positive light on gambling (because there's nothing positive about it), but sometimes I wonder if a "successful" gambler sitting at a table in Las Vegas has more sense than some Christians.

SO WHAT DO WE NEED TO DO?

First, if you're interested in seeing another generation after yours experience God in a vibrant way, you've got to start asking hard questions. Ask yourself, "Am I ready to get down to the business God has for me?"

I'm not one to avoid asking questions. In fact, I believe questioning everything in life keeps us on the cutting edge of imitating, believing, and becoming the people God wants us to be.

Sometimes we have to ask ourselves how we got where we are today, and in order to understand our failures, we've got to have the freedom to ask questions and get ready for hard answers. Future Christian generations deserve nothing short of us understanding how to lead and disciple people to know the mysteries God has for us. Have you ever heard the phrase, "It's like the blind leading the blind"? If we don't take a proactive stance on how to disciple people, how can we expect to change any of today's statistics?

As we try and figure out the hardest parts of the Christian faith, let's not forget that tact plays an important role in our investigation. There are right ways to ask questions and wrong ways to ask questions. You can ask questions just to make somebody look stupid, but that doesn't help you find truth.

You can ask questions to set someone up to answer a certain way, but your motive is clearly wrong.

You can virtually run your own debate as you ask questions even when you know the answer and look like an intelligent snob.

Or you can ask a sincere, nonthreatening investigative question meant for no other purpose than to add meaning to your spiritual discovery.

I'm not in the business of making someone look stupid, so even if the questions are a bit tongue-in-cheek, please know that's how they're intended. So, for my first *big* one...

WHAT DOES IT MEAN TO MAKE A DISCIPLE?

Jesus commands it. They were his final words on earth, so they hold a bit of weight in any debate. "Go and make disciples" (Matthew 28:19). Many of your Bibles even have it in bold type: **The Great Commission**. But what does that mean?

Jesus made disciples by inviting them into a close relationship of discovery. It was a lifestyle, and he didn't reserve the right to be a disciple for those who were morally squeaky-clean. He invited fishermen, tax collectors, even murderous liars to sit as his feet and learn about the greatest gift the God of the universe promised humanity. He invited them into a relationship to discover the meaning of imitating his life. He helped them discover belief and ultimately planned for their transformation into true, real-life followers.

No prayer meetings.

No Bible studies.

In fact, the first place in the Bible the disciples actually ever prayed is when they asked Jesus to teach them to pray. (Coincidentally, in response, he just rattled off the most quoted prayer of all time, the "Lord's Prayer," in Luke 11:2-4.)

But for some reason we continue to preach the mission over and over again as...making disciples equals getting as many people in the world as possible to say a little prayer. Then somehow we think we've done our duty for the gospel. But we've forgotten.

We've forgotten that Christianity isn't a business. It's not a numbers game. Just because someone has chalked up a large number of people who decided to follow Jesus through a message or some conversation doesn't necessarily mean those people are disciples.

Judas said he would follow Jesus, but you'd be hard-pressed to find *any* theologically sound professor make the case that Judas believed in Jesus. It can't be as simple as a line at the end of a sermon. It's just not like that.

And so what if you shared your faith and convinced someone to say the "sinner's prayer"? That doesn't make you a disciple-maker if the other person's beliefs and actions don't line up with his "confession."

The apostle James has a straight-from-the-heart way of putting this: "You believe that God is one, you do well. Even the demons believe—and shudder!" (James 2:19)

I'm proposing that discipleship *must be more than confession.*

Q: WHERE ARE ALL THE SPIRITUAL GIANTS? A: OUT STARTING BIBLE STUDIES

One of the first things they teach you in some Christian circles is that when you get saved, you need to start a Bible study. Leaders told me throughout my spiritual journey that if I wanted to serve God, I needed to go out and gather people together and start a meeting. A Bible study!

I don't want to get too far into my criticism before acknowledging that Bible study is very important. We've got to understand the Word of God in all its brilliance, know that reading the Bible illuminates God's character to us. We must be familiar with the teachings of Jesus in order to imitate them—but too many of us have forgotten the reason the Bible study exists.

Unfortunately, many Bible studies today are filled with lots of fun and a little Bible, if any. Many center around pizza, hanging out at someone's house, and talking about the latest TV shows—but they have no real time in the Bible. Why do we concentrate on Bible studies with food and fun, and then try to follow up with a mediocre stab at our original intention? The Bible study has become an item on a spiritual "feel good" list that we can check off, but in reality it does little to help us understand the meaning behind God's word.

IT'S NOT DISCIPLESHIP; IT'S A COUNTRY CLUB

I often wonder what good we're doing with this pseudo-country-club Christianity when we get together for pizza, but the business at hand is reduced to little more than an iota of knowing who God is. After all, isn't knowing God supposed to be the whole point? Isn't the purpose of a Christian group meeting to discuss the Bible and create a place to invite people to a better understanding of who God is?

I believe the best way of countering the country-club mentality is to begin to show people what a real Bible study looks like. Instead of starting a group just for the sake of passing a spiritual litmus test, let's start meetings that make a difference.

WHAT IF?

What if, instead of another group meeting in the week, we actually spent time understanding God? We could use the Bible as our anchor, but what if Bible study was part study and part living?

We could reinvent the Christian community as we consider the truths we learn from the Bible, discern

God's intention, and then turn around and commit a certain time of our group meetings to pursuing crucial principles in our lives. We could begin to become followers of Jesus and use the imitation stage to bridge theoretical knowledge to real-life living.

I wonder if Christian leaders today have convinced us that the point of the meeting is the meeting itself instead of giving us a clear vision of the outcome of every meeting. What if we took it to the next level?

Every meeting you go to called "Bible study" should challenge you. It should cause you to think about deep ideas. Instead of wrapping it up like a sitcom in 30 minutes or less, what if your Bible study moved you for days or weeks or—perish the thought—months at a time?

I know in my life, the most significant Bible studies have been those when I don't leave knowing the answers, but rather, when I leave asking more questions. When I continue the momentum of knowing God, I move down the spiritual highway. If I feel like I've got it all together, it stops my spiritual life.

There's no journey.

There's no new discovery.

There's no new revelation.

It's just stale Bible reading.

But let's not get too far ahead without recognizing the cold, hard facts. Some things found in the Bible are qualitative, meaning they qualify the setting or the surroundings of an event, while others are quantitative and reveal the innermost parts of our spiritual beings.

Jesus was born in Bethlehem.

Fact.

Easy to understand.

Easy to qualify.

Hard to imitate.

Try to contemplate Jesus as God and man at the same time. The Bible says, "God was pleased to have all his fullness dwell in him" (Colossians 1:19). Imagining sitting with Jesus while he was on the earth conjures a rich romantic ideal. As I think about him as a man, imitating him seems relatively easy, but to imitate him as God is a difficult notion.

I can see Jesus, in my mind's eye, lying in the manger. I can see him feeding the 5,000. I can visualize the pain he felt on the cross. But Jesus was certainly more than those images.

He was the only God-man who ever existed.

He was, before the manger.

He is, after the cross.

He sits on the throne of heaven at the right hand of God the Father.

How do you understand a concept by merely using language?

We've got to experience the majesty of God. We've got to let the universal God permeate to the very core of who we are. You can't know God the Creator of the universe by simply describing the Creator; you have to experience God.

If you leave a Bible study without a series of questions about how to combine the truth you learn with everyday life, then your meeting has been nothing more than reductional religion. It's just a think tank of theology rather than a proactive discovery.

If we want to be a part of a generation of God-fearing, God-loving people, we've got to reinvent the way we learn about God. If you want to be a part of duplicating your faith and helping to create a whole body of believers in your community, then you need to take a serious look at the purpose of your meetings and the outcome of their existence.

If your behavior doesn't change after you approach God's Word, then ask yourself, "Do I really believe enough to become?"

THE IMPORTANCE OF PURPOSE

Purpose is the bullseye of anything you do. It's the reason you engage in life. If you have purpose in life, then you wake up in the morning. If you don't, then you lie in bed wondering about what your purpose is.

The overwhelming response to Rick Warren's book, *The Purpose Driven Life*, is no coincidence. Warren outlines the way Christians can stop running the rat race of life and get behind something with deep meaning—with purpose. He illuminates the dark corners of life so we can say, "Yeah, I want to follow something that will last." And his "40 Days of Purpose" will go down as a great revolution in a generation of Christians.

The meaning of life has been at the center of philosophical conversation since the beginning of thought.

What are we doing here?

Why are we doing it that way?

Is there a better way?

Purpose is crucial in your mission to duplicate your faith. (Don't skip this next part! It's important.)

Ask yourself three simple questions:

1. *Why do I want to disciple someone?* Is it for me, or is it for them?

Discipleship is a spiritual discipline. It's not so you can walk around your campus, or your job for that matter, and act spiritual. If you don't think you're ready to share your faith in an honest way then take some time away from this book. Sit down and ask yourself hard questions about your motives. Too many Christians are trying to win God's approval through discipleship, and they forget the meaning behind influencing those around them to know more about Jesus. Why do you want to do this?

2. *What do I want the outcome to be?* Do you want to learn more about God? Do you want to learn more about leadership? Do you want to help someone else's spiritual journey?

The outcome is as important as your initial motive or purpose. What do you want this "discipleship" relationship to look like in a month? Two months? A year? Is it merely another meeting with a friend to check off your spiritual checklist? Do you think God is going to be impressed because you have breakfast with your friend?

Of course not. Take some time to decide where you want to be at the end of your journey. Maybe the destination looks like this...

a. You've memorized a section of Scripture.

b. You've tackled a particular theological problem, and you've done pretty good research to establish a point.

c. You've developed a system of beliefs about "X" that help you walk the hallway of school today.

Or maybe it's any combination. Rest assured, there's no magical destination. There's no "right way" to disciple someone. Think of it like this: Discipleship is a relationship with someone else working on hard issues of faith.

Discipleship is life-on-life learning.

Discipleship is growing together in the knowledge of God.

I was recently in a meeting with a group of friends discussing the issue of discipleship. After I suggested some of these methods, one guy raised his hand and said, "Andy, how can teenagers disciple teenagers? What if they don't have all the answers?" *What?!*

That's precisely why I'm writing this book—not to give you the answers to every theological question, but to encourage you to ask more. I have no intention of outlining your spiritual journey for you; I merely want you to think about the way you know God.

It's okay if you don't have all the answers. No human being does. And it doesn't reduce God to anything less than what God is—a mystery. God is a mysterious spiritual being who loves you enough to provide a way for you to know him. As you set up your goal for the destination, don't be afraid to not know. That's the exciting part of learning.

3. *How do I want to duplicate what I believe?* Do you want to meet? Do you want to have conversations on AIM, or MySpace, or Facebook? What is the mode by which you want to learn?

The last question in the process of duplication is *how?* How are you going to develop this relationship with the person with whom you're going to share your faith? Some people like breakfast before school. Some people like ice cream afterward. I've seen some groups meet in their homes. I've watched teenagers duplicate across the country via e-mail, and I've seen international teenagers pick a certain book to read and talk about. There's nothing magical about it. You just have to decide how you're going to set up the rules—and stick to them.

If you're going to meet at Starbucks before school, then don't miss it. Don't compromise your meeting. Make sure it's the most important part of your week. That way, as consistency begins to pay off, you're going to find a rich, abundant relationship with your new disciple.

These questions will help you qualify your reason for doing what you're about to do. They will keep you on task and continue to help you bring the discussion back to the target. It will be easy to chase rabbits down the rabbit trail as you discuss things like pain, sovereignty, and God's love, and I encourage you to chase them all. However, having a clear guide or direction is going to help you stay on task.

THE GENUINE IMPORTANCE OF DUPLICATION

Paul used the metaphor of the body as he described the group of believers we call Christians. It's *crucial* that you take the time to reinvent yourself in order for the body to function. If you can grasp the global implications of your decision to help someone else know Jesus in an intimate way; if you can be encouraged to help someone who has gifts and talents to use them to love God with all her heart; if you can, in essence, get over the idea that you're the most important person in God's global kingdom, you're going to experience this faith called Christianity—in a vibrancy you can't even dream of.

For you to share the most important part of life with someone else is the greatest gift you can give a person, and as you share this foundational information and struggle through the truths found in the Bible, you're going to build an enormous love for God, because you're going to see how vast God's love for you is.

In my years as a youth leader, I've found the high-est-impact times in my spiritual life are when I'm in the battle with my friends. When I struggle through a certain passage or a certain idea, the hair on the back of my neck stands up, and something in my soul screams out, *I get it!* But, if I minimize my experience with God to only an individual faith, I feel defeated. I feel worth-less. I feel as though the purpose for my life isn't being fulfilled. This isn't to say I don't have rich times with God by myself, but there's definitely something excit-ing about sharing your life with someone else in the same phase of life as you are.

This Christian life is all about community. It's all about sharing the mountaintops of success with some-one so you can celebrate together. And in some kind of paradoxical way, this Christian life is also about walk-ing through the deepest canyons of despair with some-one who cares about your innermost soul.

DEVELOPING AN ETERNAL PERSPECTIVE

I want to encourage you. I want to exhort you. I want you to know the journey on which you're about to embark is one that's going to develop you in a *deep* way. There will be times of discouragement. There will be times you feel like you've failed. There will be times when you wonder why you're doing what you're doing, or how someone can hear such rich truth and walk away as if he's never heard it. But don't let it get to you.

Christian artist Ray Boltz used to sing a song called "Thank You." It's about going to heaven and meeting people you guided and helped and prayed for during your life:

YOU USED TO TEACH MY SUNDAY SCHOOL

WHEN I WAS ONLY EIGHT

AND EVERY WEEK YOU WOULD SAY A PRAYER

BEFORE THE CLASS WOULD START

AND ONE DAY WHEN YOU SAID THAT PRAYER

I ASKED JESUS IN MY HEART.

That's the perspective we need—one that understands even a small prayer in an elementary Sunday school class may just help someone know the love God has for him. Who knows? The journey you're about to take may just help someone understand how to love God with all her heart and thus be able to experience God in this life and have hope for a life to come. Ultimately, we disciple in order to share God's infinite love with those we care about the most. So get ready...cut and run!

TRANSFER OF INFORMATION

"Go and make disciples…"

—MATTHEW 28:19

Have you ever wanted to learn how to play an instrument? What about starting a hobby? Have you ever wanted to paint oil on canvas, or build model airplanes, or play real music? My piano teacher used to tell me, "Practice makes perfect." And she was right. If you want to learn an art or a craft, you have to spend time learning basic skills. If you want to learn how to paint, it requires a certain training regimen to be able to see shades of color, luminescence, and dimensional objectivity. If you want to learn how to play the piano, you have to understand where the keys are and how they sound together. The only way to learn these skills is from someone who knows them already.

Very few people merely pick up skills like prodigies. Athletes need coaches, musicians need teachers, and actors need instructors. Any craft requires a transfer of information to help the student understand all the parts of the game, every piece of the instrument, or every square inch of the stage.

I went to college to be an actor. I don't know why, but the thrill of the stage enticed me from a very early age, and I can remember acting in small high school productions, thinking, *I could do this for a living.* So when I went off to the university, it was a natural major.

I started by taking an introduction-to-acting class, and I fell in love with the craft. I enjoyed creating real-life characters to tell various stories to live audiences. It was a thrill to me. I'll never forget the excitement when my acting coach came to me and said, "Hey, you're pretty good at this. Would you like to learn how to act?"

I was overwhelmed with excitement! I couldn't believe someone saw something in me that might amount to something. I immediately got on the campus computer and began signing up for my classes the following semester. And for the next three years, I lived in the theater. I went to class at eight in the morning, took a lunch break, and often didn't get back to my apartment until after midnight.

I read all the acting books I could get hold of. I watched as many great actors perform as time permitted. I was obsessed with reading more and more plays, and each step of the way, I invited the acting coaches to train me. I wanted to be the best darn actor I could be.

A funny thing happened as I spent time learning the craft of acting. I started becoming an actor. Everything

I thought about was acting. Everything I talked about was acting. Every movie I saw, I tried to think through and understand how and why the director made the choices he made. I became that which I thought about the most.

The same thing happens when new Christians long to know the basic truths of the Bible. They need someone to come alongside and help them understand basic truths of the faith. They need someone to go back to the basics and mentor them through the tough times lying ahead in the dark.

It's no surprise Jesus told his disciples, "Go and make disciples of all nations" (Matthew 28:19). He recognized the need for new believers to go through a series of friendships along life's road to encourage them in their growth. Very few will ever "get it" from one event. Life experience and a little training go a long way.

As I watched the most recent *Star Wars* episode, *Revenge of the Sith*, I noticed a Christian principle: Young Obi-Wan Kenobi spends every waking moment with the teenage Anakin Skywalker. They live together, eat together, travel together, and fight together. Young Anakin always looks for the lead from Obi-Wan, not because he can't make the decisions, but because he longs to learn the ways of the Jedi. After a certain number of battles and a vote from the Jedi Council, Anakin is supposed to become a Jedi master, ready to teach another young would-be warrior.

If we follow Jesus' teachings, the life of a Jedi isn't that different from our own. We must transfer the information from one generation to another in order for the Christian faith to survive. According to Josh McDowell's book, *The Last Christian Generation*:

- 63 percent of teenagers don't believe Jesus is the son of the one true God;

- 58 percent of teenagers believe all faiths teach equally valid truths;

- 51 percent of teenagers don't believe Jesus actually rose from the dead;

- 65 percent don't believe Satan is a real entity; and

- 68 percent don't believe the Holy Spirit is a real person.

Why is there a generation of teenagers being denied these basic fundamental building blocks of the faith?

Because we've failed to recognize the importance of living life together. We've started to compartmentalize every piece of our lives, including our spiritual lives, and our culture denies the fact that we need each other. Life today is all about self. "Give me what I want when I want it, and then I'll be okay." "I can make it on my own." "I pulled myself up by my bootstraps and became the success I am today."

We used to have time to sit and talk. Talk about class. Talk about tests. Talk about movies. Talk about music. But today we don't have time to stop. Our conversations are limited to whatever fits into a text message on a cell phone. Our letters are a conglomeration of syntax no English professor could ever decode.

Is there a problem with technology? No! Technology allows the beginnings of relationships to form. It helps us communicate to people across oceans. It's an incredible tool. But we must not let our access to technology rob us of the power of living life with friends.

Duplication across the Internet is a powerful way to start relationships. I've even learned how to hone my own journey by conversations over MySpace, e-mail, and Facebook. They're incredible communication tools. But remember, quick notes over the technology highway can't ever replace good old-fashioned face-to-face conversations. Be careful not to let convenience rule over quality when it comes to the message. This journey takes time.

It takes time to explore basic issues of the faith.

It takes time to let those issues sink into your heart.

It takes time to move from imitation to belief.

It takes time to become a true follower of Jesus.

It also takes guts.

Discipleship today isn't something that comes naturally to all people. It takes a bit of moxie to sit with someone and discuss the relevant parts of faith. It takes a bit of courage to ask your pastor, "How do you know there's a God in the universe?" Certainly there's a risk of appearing like a heretic and getting thrown out of the church, but let's be honest: It's a necessary part of learning. We mustn't be afraid to make our faith relevant to our lives. Don't let fear cripple you from asking hard questions.

Sometimes we're afraid we don't know the answers to all our duplication partners' questions, so it's better we remain silent on tough issues. Some believe it's up to them to find their own way in the Christian faith. Why not? If you've come this far, surely someone else can catch up, right?

Wrong! It's not about catching up. Discipleship isn't another check box on the list of "good Christian" things to do. It's life! It's the only way one believer can communicate truth to another believer, who then can figure out if the theory holds water. Discipleship is as much about understanding truth yourself as it is about you teaching truth to someone else.

The tidal wave building across this country at the start of the millennium is one not seen since the great awakenings of the early 1900s. For the first time in my life, I'm witnessing believers who long to know how to figure out if God is real or not. They're tired of programs. They're tired of singing the same old songs. It's time we lived life one-on-one. Believer to believer. It's time for meaningful relationships to take center stage so the world can see if we really believe what we say we believe.

My hope is that this book will encourage you to imitate Jesus. I hope there are a few areas where you can learn something and turn around to be a coach to someone else. It doesn't matter if you're 13 or 30; everybody needs somebody to come beside them and walk through the different phases of life.

Let's get this party started!

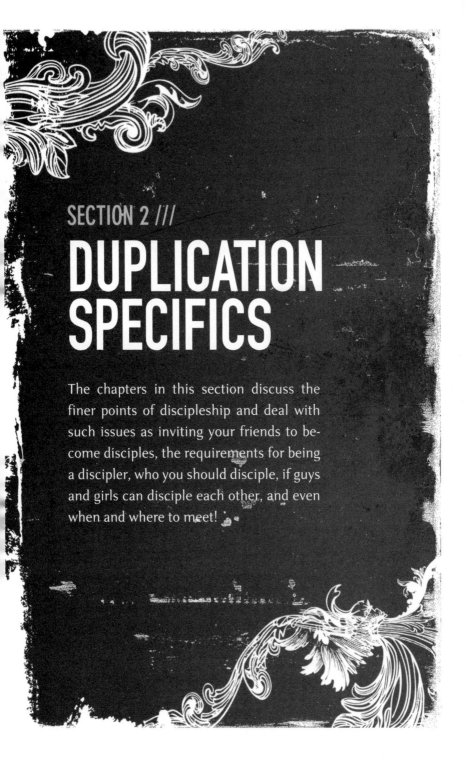

DUPLICATION SPECIFICS

The chapters in this section discuss the finer points of discipleship and deal with such issues as inviting your friends to become disciples, the requirements for being a discipler, who you should disciple, if guys and girls can disciple each other, and even when and where to meet!

WHY DO YOU ASK ME THAT?

As iron sharpens iron, so one man

sharpens another.

—PROVERBS 27:17

The principles of duplication are simple. *Imitate. Believe. Become.* Those are the three tenets of knowing your faith and then sharing your faith with a friend. They are the foundation of creating a process of believers unashamed of the gospel (Romans 1:16). In order for you to make your faith your own, you must ask questions. You must seek to know answers.

You can't simply stay in the first phase of imitation, or you risk your spiritual life becoming no more than make-believe being played by a puppet or a mime.

You have to stretch yourself and begin to believe. Belief is the second brick in the process of understanding God's wisdom and knowledge, but if you simply stay in the belief phase, you'll do nothing about what you believe.

When you allow the teachings of Jesus to fill your soul, you'll be well on your way to obeying his commandments and thus loving the God who created you. But that's not the end.

God didn't create you to be a lone ranger here on earth, simply focusing on your own spiritual journey. You need people in your life to show you who you really are.

I remember the first time my acting teacher videotaped a performance. We went back into the green room to watch the film, and I was totally embarrassed. All the notes he gave me to help my craft of acting were detailed on the video. I had a chance to observe, for myself, what others were seeing when I took the stage.

Something happens when a second party has access to your life. You find it hard to justify certain behavior, and you begin to open up to the possibility that you aren't exactly representing the person you want to be to the world around you.

WHY DO I NEED SOMEONE KEEPING ME ACCOUNTABLE?

Most Christian organizations call this partnership *accountability*. Even writing the word on this page scares me. But accountability is simply letting someone into your life to help keep account of your actions.

Accountability is not intended to be a police force. It's not a relationship where you invite someone into your life, and he or she can air out all your dirty laundry. All relationships I've had like that ended up in failure.

I don't want *anyone* to know I'm not perfect, so instead of the relationship being fruitful, I tend to wind up hiding my mistakes. I can hide anything from anyone I want.

I hate that about myself, but it's true.

If you and I were accountability partners, and we set up a time when I shared all the times I messed up, I would eventually get tired of sharing all my sins. I can put on a smile when I hurt inside. I can dance around certain questions to make myself look good, and so can you. We're masters at it.

We don't want anyone to know what's really going on down deep in our souls. It's embarrassing, and some people think it tends to be more work to let someone in so close.

But what if we redefined the word *accountability*? What if accountability became less of a police force, and more of a celebration of life?

I have an easier time sharing with someone if I can trust that he has my best interests in mind. If I feel like someone is truly helping me to get better, then the times when life is dirty become easier to share because I know the person sitting across the table is truly interested in seeing me succeed.

Sometimes people get into relationships clouded with mistrust, and the partnerships that fail usually have several episodes of shady friendship. It's vitally important to choose someone to be a part of your life who can celebrate your life. You need to make sure you have a high level of trust with the person you're sharing with.

The Bible talks of this partnership like that of iron. When iron sharpens iron (Proverbs 27:17), there are sparks, but the end result is a shapely sculpture refined to perfection.

WHO SHOULD BE MY ACCOUNTABILITY PARTNER?

Batman had Robin.

Thelma had Louise.

Romy had Michelle.

Jackie Chan has Chris Tucker.

Partnerships are common in our entertainment world, which is an interesting cultural phenomenon as it relates to modern Christian living.

Paul had Barnabas. Timothy had Paul. The apostles had each other. David had Jonathan. The Bible is filled with people whose relationships were hard, but they helped each other when life got difficult.

When you start searching for your own account-ability partner, here are a few items to check off before you invite him or her into your life.

1. Do you look up to him?

2. Do you respect her?

3. Can you trust him?

4. Are you willing to share private failure with her?

5. Can you celebrate together the abundant life Jesus came to give?

6. Is he wise?

7. Does she know how to speak your language (and I don't mean English or Spanish)?

8. Are you both heading in the same direction spiritually?

9. Do you have common interests?

10. Can you qualify your growth as it relates to your time with him?

It's not a decision to be taken lightly. Take some time to search for someone who can truly help you sharpen your spiritual life like iron sharpens a sword. I promise, when you begin this life with someone alongside you, it becomes less confusing, and your spiritual journey begins to take on the characteristics God intended.

Go out and find someone to grow with!

CHAPTER FIVE

I'VE GOT TO TELL MY FRIENDS...

May we shout for joy over your salvation, and

in the name of our God set up our banners!

—PSALM 20:5 (ESV)

I love taking students on trips around the planet to share their faith. It's a teacher's greatest joy to watch the proverbial light bulb go off in a student's mind. The "aha!" moment is a thrill, and watching students catch the passion to share their faith is one of the greatest moments in life.

I don't want them to share because I told them to or somehow convinced them to share. I want to see if there's a deep-seated desire to share, because in sharing what you believe to be true, you can rest assured it goes deeper than a fad or a moment in time. If you're willing to share something as true in your own life, chances are you know it's true and have begun to believe it.

GO AND MAKE NEW DISCIPLES

Go therefore and make disciples of all
nations, baptizing them in the name of the
Father and of the Son and of the Holy Spirit,
teaching them to observe all that I have
commanded you. And behold, I am with you
always, to the end of the age.

—MATTHEW 28:19-20 (ESV)

The world calls it proselytizing, and for all practical purposes, what they're referring to is not the right way to disciple someone. Jesus didn't tell people to go out on the street corner and slander people because of their sin in hopes that they'd come to repentance.

He didn't even ask you to argue with someone until he comes to a realization of salvation.

No, Jesus said, "Go." Go to all nations and make disciples.

Today, making disciples looks a lot different than it did even 15 or 20 years ago. People aren't as compelled to listen to someone ranting and raving about sin in the world and prophecy of doom and destruction.

We've moved into a time period when the general public is longing for someone to live what she says. They want to check you out personally and make sure you're the real deal before they let you into their spiritual worlds. Some people don't think they need God, while others are simply ignorant of the fact that God exists.

Some Christians think you have to be an old, wise sage to speak into the lives of others. Don't be fooled—you don't have to be 60 years old to start discipling someone; you can start today. Paul told Timothy, "Let no one despise you for your youth, but set the believers an example in speech, in conduct, in love, in faith, in purity. Until I come, devote yourself to the public reading of Scripture, to exhortation, to teaching. Do not neglect the gift you have, which was given you by prophecy when the council of elders laid their hands on you. Practice these things; devote yourself to them, so that all may see your progress. Keep a close watch on yourself and on the teaching. Persist in this, for by so doing you will save both yourself and your hearers" (1 Timothy 4:12-16, ESV).

When you set out to disciple someone, all you need is simply to be *one* step ahead of the person you're teaching. As you go through this book, each chapter is dedicated to preparing you to take one step forward. You'll have plenty to talk about if you simply look up the Scriptures and combine your reading with a little study on that particular issue.

Go and find someone who respects you. Find someone who looks up to you. Find someone who would be excited to sit down over a cup of coffee, or a slice of pizza, and talk about how to know God's will in his life. It's the most rewarding part of being a Christian, because it's true to Jesus' commandment.

SET UP NEW MEETING TIMES FOR YOUR DISCIPLE

Meetings are fun, but they're way more fun if you're doing something you enjoy.

You don't have to meet at a dingy old school building to begin your discipleship lessons.

Go to Starbucks.

Go to McDonald's.

Go to the skate park.

Go do something you both enjoy, and on the way, take a few minutes to talk about the issues you want to talk about.

The best discipleship meetings are coupled with life activities. I love riding bikes, working on landscaping, or just hanging out at the house over dinner. In the midst of activity, I find places where whoever I'm focused on at the time can ask hard questions.

It doesn't have to be some formal meeting where you check the spiritual checklist so you can say to God,

"Look at me—I'm making disciples." It's just a part of life. If you like to watch basketball, go ahead and invite your person to the game.

If you like to paint pottery, make it a point to invite the person you're discipling to hang with you at the pottery studio.

One of many things Jesus did well was invite the 12 disciples to come and live with him. He didn't preach from afar; he met with them exactly where they were. Don't be afraid to live life together. It's so much more fun than trying to live like a lone ranger.

WHAT DOES YOUR DUPLICATION PARTNER NEED TO KNOW?

The first session in any relationship should be dedicated to getting to know someone. Ask about what she likes, what he's into, and what issues she'd like to study. Make a note of the needs *they* have.

So many people try to disciple from the standpoint of, "I have what you need, and you'll like it."

Recently a friend of mine asked me about how I teach teenagers through a spiritual formation process, and when I thought about it, it was a simple question to answer. I just use all of life's experiences, all my education, and all my compassion to meet students where students are. I usually don't have a set agenda, unless it's required. I feel like it's my goal to help students where they are, not try to force them to understand something I think. And so, they keep coming back.

The biggest mistake Christians make in sharing their faith is thinking they have to know all the answers right now! They think they have to have some sort of moral platform to bring people up to where they are.

Jesus didn't say, "Go and answer all the critics," did he? Jesus said, "Go and make disciples," and if we're supposed to mirror our disciple-making after what Jesus did, then it only makes sense that we take a second and review.

He lived with them.

He traveled with them.

He ate with them.

He drank with them.

He celebrated victory with them.

He mourned in defeat with them.

He taught them.

He watched them.

They watched him.

He challenged them.

He pointed them to a higher calling.

He sent them out.

Today pick one. Pick one of those attributes as you consider who to disciple. Who'll be the person to whom you're going to transfer all your knowledge, so she, too, can know the saving power of Jesus?

Once you've decided who it is, just pick one characteristic of Jesus to focus on, and plan how you're going to work toward it. Discipleship isn't something that happens overnight. It takes time—lots of quality time. But in the end the return on investment is well worth the time you spend.

THE WONDER OF MULTIPLICATION

2+2=4...2x2=4...2+3=5...2x3=6

I n the early stages of math, the numbers are the same, but then they start deviating. If I multiply, I can get more results with the same numbers than if I add them.

I know it's a remedial kindergarten math lesson, but think about it. If you can multiply and get more results, why get so hung up on addition?

IT'S SIMPLE MATH, MY DEAR WATSON

I realize talking about discipleship in terms of mathematical theory sounds a little crazy, but I believe it's essential. We need to begin focusing on the fact that one person isn't going to spread the word around the globe. Three people aren't going to do it. Not 300. Not 3,000. We have to be more strategic in our thinking. There are 6 billion people in the world, and if they're going to have an inkling of a chance, we need to start thinking globally, exponentially, and bigger than we're thinking now.

One of the kids in the local high school decided he had a vision to share the gospel with every high school student before he graduated.

Well, there are more than 1,500 high school students in the school. If he met with one student every day of the year, including the summer, it was going to take him a little more than four years to share. But what if he missed a day? What if he couldn't reach someone that day? What if he got sick? The whole plan would have self-destructed!

But what if he deputized some of the other students to be sharers as well? Could he do it quicker if he had a little help? Surely there were some other Christians in the school who took Jesus' words seriously and desired to share their faith, too.

That's exactly what my friend found. He identified 25 students who shared his vision to spread the gospel in his school. Think about that! Now instead of every day for four years, he now had it whittled down to 60 students per. They only had to share their faith with 60 students in order to reach the aforementioned goal. It's all about multiplication!

KEEP PLUGGING AWAY

It's the same way in discipleship. You can't do it on your own; you need help. If you're serious about seeing a next-generation revolution, you must implore those you're discipling to go out and share with others. Just think about it. If you meet with someone for six months, and then that guy you met with meets with someone else for the next six while you pick a new disciple, in less than a year, there will be four of you. If you continue for two years, you'll have 16 people involved in your small group.

Can you imagine what would happen if you spent another year just like that? One person sharing life and faith with another person, so she could turn around and share with someone else? You'd have more than 63 people involved in this discipleship idea.

Multiplication always works faster and more effectively than addition. You can't possibly watch your sphere of influence grow to 63 people by yourself. Can you imagine trying to have 63 meetings a week, or making 63 phone calls, or even trying to figure out where each of the 63 people are on their own spiritual journeys? You must implore the people you spend time with to go and find someone else to pour their lives into.

It's amazing to think about the 12 disciples who walked with Jesus in a small country by the Mediterranean Sea. Most of them were just fishermen, until Paul was added to the ministry—then they had a murderer onboard.

Think about it. Twelve blue-collar workers and a murderer changed the world, because they saw the value of multiplication. They knew their boundaries, and they had a *great* vision to watch the gospel circumvent the globe.

How can you do that?

TRUST GOD

You've got to trust God. You've got to pick someone to invest your time in, and then trust God for the next person.

Too many Christians act like the gatekeepers of the Bible, when actually God never intended one person to be the only voice. In fact, check out the churches that sprang up all over Asia Minor within 100 years of Jesus' ascension. The churches of Colossae, Ephesus, Galatia, and Thessalonica were all made up of people who wanted to know how to love God more.

They didn't have one person directing their entire journey. Paul encouraged them, and he can be given credit for starting some of those places, but he couldn't preach every Sunday. He couldn't minister to the thousands of people in each one of those congregations.

Paul had to rely on other overseers to get the job done. He had to trust God's providence and wisdom to put the right person in the job at the right time.

Trust Jesus. Trust that he's going to bring someone into your life who's excited about the concept of multiplication.

Wouldn't it be a radical revolution if we saw teenagers all over the globe searching for God in a way that's honest and true because you decided to trust God to bring you a few guys or girls to disciple?

Wouldn't it be cool to watch as thousands of people came to know the saving, loving grace God offers humanity, for free—all because you took a chance at helping someone start knowing what he believes and why he believes it?

I don't think the vision is too far off.

In fact, I think it can be done. And, with your help, I believe teenagers can disciple teenagers all over the globe.

Are you ready to take the challenge?

CHAPTER SEVEN

WHAT ARE THE REQUIREMENTS FOR BEING A DISCIPLER?

The saying is trustworthy: If anyone aspires to the office of overseer, he desires a noble task. Therefore an overseer must be above reproach, the husband of one wife, sober-minded, self-controlled, respectable, hospitable, able to teach, not a drunkard, not violent but gentle, not quarrelsome, not a lover of money. He must manage his own household well, with all dignity keeping his children submissive, for if someone does not know how to manage his own household, how will he care for God's church? He must not be a recent convert, or he may become puffed up with conceit and fall into the condemnation of the devil. Moreover, he must be well thought of by outsiders, so that he may not fall into disgrace, into a snare of the devil.

—1 TIMOTHY 3:1-7 (ESV)

DIE TO YOURSELF

The first step in being an effective discipler is to understand that you die to all your rights. It's a confusing notion, especially since we live in the freedom capital of the world, America. But realizing you no longer have the right to focus on yourself anymore is a hard step to make for some people; however, it's an essential notion.

To be above reproach means you can't just do whatever you want to do. When you're trying to be a leader and influence others, there's a certain level of integrity you have to maintain in order for people to follow you. If you want others to follow God, you need to follow God. If you want others to obey Jesus' teachings, you need to obey Jesus' teachings. If you want people to be excited about godly things, you need to be excited.

To be respectable, hospitable, and able to teach are basic qualifications of a discipler. You can't just fly off the handle because you feel like it anymore. You have to respect people. You need to understand that the words you use and your tone of voice are vitally important to the ear of the person listening to whatever it is you have to say, and you need to be careful.

This isn't rocket science, either. You know how you want to be treated; just treat people like you want them to treat you. Don't be condescending. Don't be vulgar. Don't think that just because you're the one who's out starting to share this amazing gift, you're above anyone else.

Discipleship is an even playing field. We're all just trying to move in the same direction, and there's no, "Well, I got there first, so I get the prize."

DON'T BE A STUMBLING BLOCK

> And he said to his disciples, "Temptations
>
> to sin are sure to come, but woe to the one
>
> through whom they come! It would be better
>
> for him if a millstone were hung around his
>
> neck and he were cast into the sea than that
>
> he should cause one of these little ones
>
> to sin."
>
> **—LUKE 17:1-2 (ESV)**

Paul encourages overseers not to be new converts. It's a simple concept. If you're a new convert, give it some time to sink in. Find someone to help you know a little about this thing called Christianity.

You don't just go out to play basketball for the first time and then all of a sudden become the team captain. It takes work. It takes time. It takes practice. And through your own practice in Christianity, you'll start building a reputation and a rapport among people.

I guarantee there are people who want someone genuine to look up to. I wouldn't have a job if it weren't the case. I don't have any magical powers. I don't live life perfectly. I have struggles just like the next guy, but the fact that I'm moving in a direction of understanding Jesus lends to me a better relationship with new believers.

If Jesus says we need to be careful about lust in our lives, be careful. It's hard to follow someone who talks a good talk, but when it comes down to the bottom line, she lives 180 degrees differently from the way she talks.

That's the main problem with most Christians trying to do it right in front of non-believers today. Everywhere I go, I ask people why they don't want to live like Jesus said to live, and they tell me, "I don't want to be a part of a religion with so many hypocrites." They have a point.

When we start taking a position of leadership and teaching, we need to be careful how we live our lives. The Bible says it would be better that a "millstone were hung around his neck...than that he should cause one of these little ones to sin." In other words, it would be better for those who lead people astray to sink to the bottom of the ocean and never be heard of again. God takes this very seriously, and it's vitally important that you take it seriously, too.

DUTY TO CONSISTENCY

> Therefore I urge you to imitate me. For this
> reason I am sending to you Timothy, my son
> whom I love, who is faithful in the Lord. He
> will remind you of my way of life in Christ
> Jesus, which agrees with what I teach every-
> where in every church.
>
> **—1 CORINTHIANS 4:16-17**

Imitation is one of the keys to discipleship. If people can see you living a life worthy of your calling, they'll be compelled to imitate you. If you decide it's okay to go out and party, they'll go out and party exponentially. If you decide it's okay to use vulgar language, they'll go out and use the same language exponentially.

My mentor told me, "Leadership is just like a duck." (I know that sounds a little strange; let me explain.)

When a hen duck has a gaggle of ducks, the little ducklings rely on their mom's leadership. They have no way to survive except by following their mother. When she eats, they eat. When she quacks, they quack. When she moves, they move.

When she swims, they swim. But if you watch them swim, they don't merely follow the mom in a straight line. Actually the ducks swim in a "V" pattern. The mother leads at the vortex of the V, while the ducklings fall in line to form the two lines following.

If the mother duck decides to go in a straight line, sometimes it takes the ducklings a little longer to get to point A because they aren't on the same straight-line pattern. They have a little ground to make up because the V gets wider and wider the farther back you go.

The same thing happens with leadership. If you decide to go from point A to point B in a straight line, it's going to take a little longer for those who follow you. Not everybody can imitate exactly how you do life. He interprets different situations differently. She decides to make decisions a little differently, and the result could be very different from the intended direction.

As a duplicator, understand that people aren't going to do life just like you, and that's okay. God gave everybody a different gift and a different way of looking at life. You're not a failure if someone decides to do it a little differently than you do. As long as she holds to the basic concepts and is "swimming in the same direction," she'll get there. Have patience, and extend grace to those who follow you.

It's what makes this patchwork quilt of humanity so interesting. Everybody brings a slightly different variation to the same truth. Their perception allows for the whole body of Christ to function (1 Corinthians

14:12). We need all types, so encourage those who are following you to be themselves. Just be careful you're not leading them away from God.

CHAPTER EIGHT

WHO SHOULD I DISCIPLE?

The youth, intoxicated with his admiration of
a hero, fails to see, that it is only a projection
of his own soul, which he admires.

—RALPH WALDO EMERSON

YOU ARE THE HERO

Our culture spends an inordinate amount of time worshiping celebrities. We want to watch them walk through the park, surf the ocean, shop, and dine at famous eateries. It's unbelievable how much emphasis is put on this strange form of idolatry.

Celebrities are just people who happen to be in the movies, play a sport well, and sing a certain song better than someone else. They have to dress just like you do. They have to eat just like you do. They have to pay bills, they have to work, and they have to live life, too. So why do we admire them so much?

Our culture decided long ago that actors, musicians, and athletes held some sort of value over the rest of our population. I just don't believe it! They're no different from you.

Let's look at it like this. Who are the celebrities in your sphere of influence? Who did you look up to when you were in first grade? What about seventh grade? Who do you look up to when you're a senior in high school?

There are heroes in your world one step away from you, just like you're one step away from someone looking up to you. No matter if you're a senior in high school or a senior executive, there are people looking to you to set the pace of life.

It might be a friend. It might be a sibling. It might be a coworker. It might just be someone on the computer looking for an attentive ear, a willing heart, and someone he can trust. Don't be fooled. You can be a hero today!

YOU PICK THE PARTNER

It's not rocket science. It's not theoretical math. It's not like basket weaving, but it's sure not as hard as most people try to make it. Picking a friend to live life with is as easy as striking up a conversation.

Take a personal inventory of the people around you.

Does anyone like to do the same stuff you do?

Do you talk?

Is there anyone who likes to go to the same places you go?

Anyone who likes the same movies you like?

Anyone who likes the same music you like?

Anyone who's secretly waiting for you to cross the lunchroom just to make the first contact?

You pick! Go initiate conversation. Just live life. The sooner you choose that person you can identify with, the sooner the barriers of insecurity are going to fall. You don't have to make a big deal about it; just be normal.

God has given us each gifts and interests. Use those gifts. Use those interests to connect with other people who do the same things.

I assure you, as soon as you connect with some-body, she is ripe for discipleship. Who knows—you might just find someone who likes to live life the same way you do. Or maybe you'll find someone who will be in your life for only a short time, and you can help him set the record straight.

The main issue is, don't be scared!

YOU ARE AN IMPORTANT PART OF THE PROCESS

God definitely has a plan, but he allows you to be an important piece of this relationship. Nobody is going to come up to you and ask to be discipled. We are an insecure people, and we don't want people to have the opportunity to reject us on so many levels. Rarely in my life do I make friends, and then out of the blue they're like, "Hey, would you mind meeting me every other week for coffee? I'd really like to know more about Jesus."

It never happens that way. The best way to get in a discipleship relationship is to look around. Take a personal inventory of people you know, or maybe people on the fringe of your life, and go to them.

Jesus didn't say *sit around and wait*. He said *go*! And going means you have to take a proactive step in identifying and initiating a friendship with someone who could be a future disciple.

Don't be scared. This is what God created you to do. I know you can do it. Go!

HOW OFTEN SHOULD WE MEET?

"Stay" is a charming word in a
friend's vocabulary.

—LOUISA MAY ALCOTT [1832-1888],
AMERICAN WRITER, REFORMER

'll never forget going off to college and wondering if I
was ever going to make any friends. I went to school
in Texas, but I grew up in Arkansas, and I knew Texas
people held tight to Texas friends.

It's something of a mystery to be in the midst of Tex-
ans as an outsider. They are truly the friendliest people
I've ever met, but it can be a bit difficult to break into
their circles of friendship. I guess it's probably that way
all over the planet.

I got to college and settled into my dorm room. I
heard a loud thumping next door and quickly ran over
to find Jake sitting in front of the biggest speakers I'd

ever seen. He was a huge guy, kind of intimidating, but he loved the same music I loved.

Instantly we were friends.

Another knock at the door, and Mike walked in. Mike was jumping up and down, obviously reveling in the fact that our next-door neighbor was going to rule the hall with this killer sound system.

We sang. We laughed. And then the three of us went off to get a burger at the local Whataburger fast-food joint.

Friends.

We developed four years of memories together and added many more friends along the way—Russ, Danny, Brian, Derek, Jeff, Dave, and Paul, just to name a few. Friendship became an easy thing. It wasn't something I had to plan, but it was something I had to be proactive about maintaining.

I didn't have to go out and search for friends, but once I made a connection, the hard part was just keeping up. Making sure we had time on the front porch was essential. Meeting for late-night girl discussions became a normal part of life, and those late-night Denny's runs were priorities. We would even sneak out to climb the buildings on campus, just to spend time together.

It didn't matter what time. It didn't matter where. Living life together happens all throughout the day.

So when you're ready and have picked that one person you'll start helping understand the stuff you know about the faith, just start living life. If it's hard to be friends, maybe you picked the wrong person. Living life should be fluid and organic, not forced and difficult.

MORNING MEETINGS

Mornings before school are great times to start the day off focusing on good stuff, but don't be fooled—mornings are no more spiritual than afternoons or evenings.

If a good cup of coffee sets you straight in the morning, then maybe this is the perfect time for you. If an egg sandwich is something you can sink your teeth into while you grapple with hard issues, then do that.

Don't force it. Mornings are good to start the day, but they're not essential.

AFTER-SCHOOL SNACKS

Sometimes right after school or right after work actually presents a better opportunity than trying to wake up early in the morning. It's not about timing, but rather, it's about consistency. Just like working out your body, to work out your spirit with a duplication partner has to have a solid foundation of consistency.

It's too easy to get busy and allow other things to invade your time. It's essential for you to carve out the times you're going to meet and make sure those times are the priority over everything. Just drop it in.

I usually take a week's calendar and start by making the things highest on my priority list essential. No meetings. No appointments. No phone calls. Nothing can interfere with those things most precious to me.

If you're serious about duplicating your faith, just make sure you have the same dedication. Nothing can invade your meetings.

ONCE-A-WEEK BIBLE STUDIES

I'm all about meeting to have several people over for Bible study. It's a great way to single out those who are most interested, but don't fall into the trap.

Some Christians try to quantify God. They think, *Goes to Bible study = good Christian*, but that's just not the case. Just because you decide to meet for a Bible study doesn't mean you're a superstar believer.

When I was in high school, my coach invited any students who were interested to join us over at his house to study the Bible. At first, I have to be honest, it was a great way to act like I was interested in the same things he was. I went simply to show off or appear godly.

It only took two or three meetings for me to come to my senses and realize I was only fooling myself.

If you're going to start a Bible study, just know there are some who are coming simply to convince themselves that they're doing the right thing. That's okay, because just like me, they might change their minds and really start getting something out of the meeting time. But don't reduce your duplication time to a big group. This is one-on-one, life-on-life ministry. Single someone out. The big groups will come in time. Now it's time for you to get real with someone. Look him in the eyes. Show her your struggles in the journey. It will be a greater impact the sooner you get over the notion of, "This is what I have to do to be a 'good' Christian."

CHAPTER TEN

CAN GUYS AND GIRLS DISCIPLE EACH OTHER?

I don't know how profitable it becomes when a couple in a dating relationship entertains the idea of mutual discipleship. I know there's the idea out there that the guy is the spiritual leader, but I've yet to discover a dating relationship that's purely discipleship. It's a complex thing, and bringing the discipline of duplication into the dating relationship is a tough nut to crack.

If you want to pray with your date, great. If you want to talk about what you're learning in your own journeys, awesome. But spiritual leadership in the Bible is reserved for a married couple.

What happens when you break up? How does a girl feel when the guy who's supposed to be her spiritual mentor all of a sudden feels as though God has told him they're supposed to break it off? It just gets tough to distinguish between the dating aspect and the spiritual growth aspect, and it can be a detriment to future growth on both sides.

BE CAREFUL OF DATING A DISCIPLE

Without turning this chapter into a dating exposé, just be wary of dating relationships that lead to "quiet time" dating. Let's be honest. Our journeys with God are intensely personal. We talk about our relationships with Jesus as he resides in our hearts. And that's a dangerous place to let in anyone else besides God.

Most dating relationships I've seen that adopt a spiritual-leadership model often turn into wild make-out sessions. It's a stereotypical statement, and not all dating relationships end up that way, but more often than not in my experience, as soon as you let someone into the final frontier of the heart, it leads to physical things. And we know God isn't pleased when we explore a physical relationship outside of commitment.

Jesus even addressed it in Matthew 5: "You have heard that it was said, 'Do not commit adultery.' But I tell you that anyone who looks at a woman lustfully has already committed adultery with her in his heart. If your right eye causes you to sin, gouge it out and throw it away. It is better for you to lose one part of your body than for your whole body to be thrown into hell" (verses 27-29).

He's serious about our thought life. He's intentional about using something so grotesque to prove a point. Sin is sin. Lust is not something God finds endearing. And when a guy shares the deepest parts of his spiritual journey with a girlfriend, he invites her heart into a relationship that has an intense possibility of becoming physical.

GUYS AND GIRLS THINK DIFFERENTLY

It's not all guys, nor is it all girls. But this is certain— guys typically think differently than girls. When I talk about dating to large groups, I'm always pressed to prove this point with a few simple questions.

Girls

a. How many of you have ever thought about your wedding day? (All the hands go up.)

b. Have you ever thought about your wedding dress? (Again, all the hands.)

c. Have you ever thought about your brides-maids' dresses? (Yet again.)

d. Have you ever thought about the flowers?

e. Have you ever thought about the music at your wedding?

f. Have you ever thought about whether you'll get married inside the church building or outside?

g. Have you ever thought about your ring? (All hands are still up.)

h. Have you ever thought about your wedding night? (Hands begin to drop. Not all, but a significant number.)

Guys

a. How many of you have ever thought about your wedding day? (None.)

b. Tuxedos? (Still no hands.)

c. Flowers? (Nope.)

d. Rings? (None.)

e. How many of you have ever thought about your wedding night? (*All* the hands go up, and the auditorium erupts.)

Guys and girls tend to think differently. Girls tend to think with emotion, and guys tend to think visually. Boys are often more wired to think about physical things. Girls are often more wired to think about personalities, sense of humor, and ideals.

This is a gross stereotype, but I've asked thousands of teenagers, and the experiment rings true. Guys think differently from girls, and that fact can play to your detriment when you're trying to establish a relationship based on discipleship.

TROUBLE CAN LURK AROUND EVERY CORNER

The enemy isn't an idiot. He's not like Wile E. Coyote. He doesn't come up with silly plans doomed for failure from the outset. He knows you. He knows how to work you. He knows where the chinks in your armor are, and he'll do anything to discourage you.

The Bible says, "The thief comes only to steal and kill and destroy" (John 10:10). He doesn't have your best interests in mind. In fact, Peter said, "Your enemy the devil prowls around like a roaring lion looking for someone to devour" (1 Peter 5:8). He's waiting to eat you alive.

So you must be guarded. You need to protect the areas of your life that you know are weak, and sexuality is a weak area for many teenagers in dating relationships. Remember, trouble can lurk around every corner, but Jesus promised, "I have come that they may have life, and have it to the full" (John 10:10).

Jesus is interested in your abundant life. He didn't come so that you would follow a certain number of rules and regulations. Jesus came to give you the most abundant life available while you're here on the planet.

Discipleship should never cross sexual borders. Because of that, the best duplicating relationships happen when a guy disciples a guy, and a girl disciples a girl. It just makes sense, and it keeps you out of trouble.

The next 18 chapters are important "FAQs" that get at crucial issues surrounding the Christian faith and living it out, so you can go to the world and feel confident about what you believe. In the end, my hope is to give you various ideas for how you can logistically set up your own coaching sessions to duplicate this Christian faith, life on life.

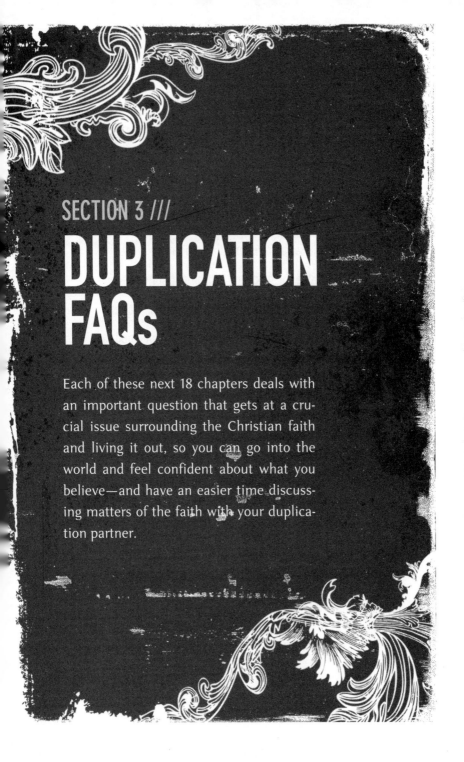

DUPLICATION FAQs

Each of these next 18 chapters deals with an important question that gets at a crucial issue surrounding the Christian faith and living it out, so you can go into the world and feel confident about what you believe—and have an easier time discussing matters of the faith with your duplication partner.

THE BIBLE...TRUE OR FALSE?

All Scripture is breathed out by God and profitable for teaching, for reproof, for correction,
and for training in righteousness, that the
man of God may be competent, equipped for
every good work.

—2 TIMOTHY 3:16-17 (ESV)

For my thoughts are not your thoughts,
neither are your ways my ways, declares the
LORD. For as the heavens are higher than the
earth, so are my ways higher than your ways
and my thoughts than your thoughts.

—ISAIAH 55:8-9 (ESV)

CHAPTER ELEVEN

I t might sound sacrilegious to even ask the question, but I find it hard to believe in something I never question. In fact, it's so risky a question that even a few Christian schools in the country haven't invited me back to speak to their students because I encourage all students to ask, "Is the Bible true or not?"

"Is it worth reading?"

"What's its purpose?"

"How does a 2,000-year-old book apply to my life?"

I know several well-meaning Christians who claim the Bible is the book of answers. If I had a quarter for every time I heard some Christian tell me, "Surely the answer to your problem is in the Bible," I'd be a very rich man. Or maybe you've heard something like, "If you'd only study the Bible, then everything will fall into place."

Sorry to burst *that* bubble, but the Bible doesn't have all of life's answers—mainly because there are things in life that occur outside the Bible's scope. The Bible doesn't mention movies, but I'd be willing to bet you've been to a movie at least once in your lifetime. And I've heard hundreds of sermons addressing the principles of movie watching in modern life. How did you know it was in "God's will" for you to go to that movie? It doesn't say anything about it in the Bible.

The Bible doesn't mention MTV, VH1, ESPN, Britney Spears, Justin Timberlake, Beyoncé, or Michael W.

Smith. It doesn't say anything implying that Christian music is helpful, while secular music isn't. So what difference does it make? Why should I live by the principles found in a book so "outdated"?

To be honest, *it makes all the difference in the world.*

You've got to know if the Bible is true or not, right? I mean, *if* the Bible can't hold a candle to truth, then what are we doing with this ridiculous book? I asked this question to a student group in Nashville, Tennessee. It didn't seem like the kids were really listening to me, so I opted for a cheap trick.

I told them they had to hold the Bible up to criticism, and if it's not true, then just stop believing it. "It would be better for you to just walk away from the faith and try doing something more fun. Just stop believing." I used all the metaphors I could think of, and then I really shocked them.

When I said, "stop believing," I clenched the little pocket Bible in my hand , wound up like I was throwing the last pitch of the World Series, and I flung that little book so hard across the gym that the pages fluttered through the air like a bird flying against a strong westward headwind. The impact was amazing. That little Bible virtually exploded against the gym wall, as if I planted some sort of bomb right there in Psalm 119. It was awesome!

Pages flew.

The binder was all torn up.

The cover was on one side of the gym, and the pages just settled quietly right there at half court.

I thought, *I got 'em now*. And, oh, how I had 'em. I looked out in the audience expecting heads to be nodding in agreement, but to my surprise...silence. I thought I had their attention, but really I had just defamed all of Christianity, because somewhere somebody told these students that the book itself is so sacred that if you threw it, you might go to hell the moment you released it from your fingers.

Certainly that day, if indeed throwing the Bible on the ground was an eternal death sentence, I was finished on the Monopoly board of life: "Do not pass Go, and do not pick up your stuff on the way out. Just fly straight into the fiery lake of sulfur." At least that's the way they were looking at me.

Some girls on the front row even looked a little sympathetic, and I could almost hear them whisper, "Poor guy. He was just trying to get our attention, but now...God's going to get him!"

One ninth grader came up to me afterward and said, "My mom always told me not to destroy my Bible. She told me to always take care of it because it's God's Word. I don't appreciate you throwing the Bible around." And she turned around and walked off.

No way to justify myself.

She was just plain mad.

You know what? As I look back on it, she was right. It is God's Word, and maybe I took that example a little far, but inside I was asking myself, *So which version would have been appropriate? The NIV, ESV, the Living Bible, the King James, the NASB...? Which one is exactly God's Word?*

Their attention was what I was after in the first place, but the endgame was their frustration that I threw *the* book, and that wasn't the point of the talk *at all.*

It's not as though God wrote *that* particular copy of the Bible, right? There's nothing sacred about any specific translation, is there?

Do people in this world really think reverence for the physical book is what God is looking for? (You can see how this can get out of hand pretty quickly.)

Let's start with a few questions you can begin with on your own journey, and maybe some questions you can share with the person you're in the duplicating group with.

WHAT KIND OF BOOK IS IT?

When you start learning how to play an instrument, it helps to have some music, right? I know, some people can just pick up a guitar and play the most magnificent pieces ever heard, but the reality for most of us is that we need some help. We need to at least have some guidelines for chord progressions, lyrics, or the overall feel of the music we're playing. The Bible is kind of like that.

It's not that every single problem you ever have will be answered in the "Good Book"; it's just that it guides Christians to understand who God is. That's the bottom line.

The Bible is merely a book that helps you know God in a more intimate way. The Bible is a collection of writings by early religious leaders who saw God in an intimate way, too.

In the Old Testament, they heard God talking; some of the New Testament writers saw God walking. And when Jesus ascended to heaven, the early church leaders helped us see the struggles they faced with this new, out-of-the-box religious idea.

It's a book written in a certain time period that contains certain transcendental truths that span time through generations. It's God's way of letting humanity in on his grandiose plan through the ages.

It's a history book.

It's a geography book.

It's a book of poetry and art.

It has a tremendous value in the sciences.

It's a romance novel, a how-to book, and a great work of philosophy all in one.

The Bible is a unique book, but we must be careful not to make an idol of the book.

It's a book, not God.

It's a picture of God, not God.

It's a collection of words and stories about God, not God.

Don't hear me say there shouldn't be a healthy reverence for the Bible. It's the source of most every theological thought we have. It's the guideline to every decision a Christian makes. But it's still just a book. It's the very idea of God written throughout the ancient days that reveals a majestic God to humanity.

WHAT THE BIBLE ISN'T

It isn't some cosmic love story from an all-loving God to you! (I get so angry when I hear that.) Some youth pastors want to make it out to be a personalized letter to each individual follower of Jesus. It's not! And the main way you can tell it wasn't written to you is...your name's not on the cover.

There are issues in the Bible that can only be answered within a cultural context of early Middle Eastern problems, and when we take those passages out of context, we totally misinterpret the authors' intentions.

For example, one of the most misused verses in the Bible is Philippians 4:13: "I can do all things through him who strengthens me" (ESV).

I've seen marathon runners wear shirts with that verse printed on them as if God is going to give them superhuman strength to finish some eternally insignificant running route.

I've watched triathletes claim God's power along the course.

I've even seen NFL players turn God into a genie that will help them win the game. Do you really think God cares about who wins the next Super Bowl? Come on. Are we so blind as to not take things into context and begin to understand the truth God is trying to tell us?

But in order to understand God, it takes work. It takes thought. It takes a little investigation. It takes a little more reading.

For instance, before you can understand the passage in Philippians, you need to read what comes before and after the verse. Specifically, when Paul writes to encourage the Philippians to be content wherever they are as they try to learn more about Jesus, he declares Jesus is the source of all completion.

Whether in hunger or pain, knowing God in an intimate way and learning how to implement God's truth in your life is the greatest goal, and if anything comes in your way, God will give you the strength to finish your journey.

We can learn principles. We can understand God's truth within the context of culture. But to say something like, "Every problem in your life can be answered if you look in the Bible," is wrong. God doesn't promise power to run the marathon. God doesn't give special skills to win the basketball game at a certain time. That's just poor interpretation.

Jesus is interested in you knowing him. He's a God full of love, and he wants you to know more about him through time. He wants you to know more about him in truth. He wants you to know more about him today, and the Bible is the key that begins to unlock those doors.

What happens when you can't find the answers to your questions?

Traditionally, if you can't find the answer, you might hear some say, "Well, you're just not looking hard enough. Keep going; God will reveal it in the Scriptures." But I don't care how long you stare at a flimsy page; God doesn't talk about cars, boats, homes, or whether you should go to McDonald's or Burger King for lunch. There's got to be more.

It's not a quick way to be "more spiritual"

I've been to hundreds of church retreats with great music, new friends, and an expectation of meeting God in a new way. Our youth group used to go to a yearly camp put on by one of the largest denominations in the world, and although I would love to say I was so spiritual and looked forward to understanding transcendental truths about God, I really just wanted to meet girls.

Something funny would happen on those trips. While I was on the prowl to meet a girl, God would somehow stir some sort of conviction of some behavior that wasn't right, and I always came away wanting to be a "better Christian."

The first step of the 12-step "how to be a better Christian" seminar is: *Read your Bible!* Right? Of course, it would be great if everyone on the planet had the Bible memorized.

King David wrote in the Psalms, "I have stored up your word in my heart that I might not sin against you" (119:11). What a goal! I took that verse to mean, if I know the Bible well enough, I can eliminate sin from my life.

So I started taking this principle literally. I started to equate the time I spent studying or memorizing Scripture to how little sin I had in my life.

If you're truly studying the Word to "store it up," not much time is left to do other things. Therefore, by the mere laws of time management, that particular technique tends to work. But it's foolish to think you're going to eradicate sin in your life just by doing Bible study.

I can tell you firsthand that the sin-management theory doesn't work. I'm not advocating a "burn all the Bibles" policy by any means. In fact, I've already stated the importance of the Bible in decision-making. That said, please understand this clearly: You won't earn a more prominent place in heaven by having more quiet times than the guy sitting next to you at the youth group retreat.

Nowhere in the Bible is there a section that helps you get a closer seat to Jesus because you're going to bring some sort of spiritual checklist with you to the judgment seat of God. If you think you're going to impress God, it's time you really dig in and read your Bible a little more carefully.

THEN WHAT'S THE PURPOSE OF THE BIBLE?

It's a unifier

Early church leaders spent decades trying to figure out which books to include in the Bible you have today. They wanted to make sure there was a unifying document that drew all believers around the table of doctrinal issues so we could have one view of the knowable triune God. They called this process canonization, and both the Old and New Testaments were subject to strict scrutiny in order to give you the book you hold in your hand today.

You can quote verses from the Bible you have today, and believers around the world will have studied that verse to varying degrees. It's a universal unifier for all believers to understand the principles of the Christian faith today.

It's an understanding

Each part of the Bible gives the reader another sneak peek at the picture of God's character and nature. In a time when God's audible voice seems to be at an all-time low, the Bible is God's voice to believers. It gives us a tremendous look at the way God created the world, how God redeemed the sin of man, and what we have to look forward to in the end when God reconciles the world back to himself.

It gives us tremendous understanding of what God's view might be concerning issues such as abortion, environmental management, and global peace. It's full of transcendent principles from a time very different from ours, and those principles continue to be true in the context of our culture.

And to be honest, that's where careful cultural critique comes in so handy. If you want to make the Bible come alive, go down to your local Jewish tabernacle when you're studying the Old Testament and start asking the rabbi about the stories, the feasts, and the celebrations of the Jewish culture. He'll be able to shed light on the shadows of cultural misunderstanding, and all of a sudden, the Old Testament will shine a bright light on your own spiritual journey.

It's a guide

In order to follow Jesus' teachings, it only makes sense that you read them. If Jesus said, "Love your neighbor as yourself" (Matthew 19:19), and you never had access to read or hear what he said, it would be difficult to live your life obeying his commandments. The Bible is a guide. It's an historic lighthouse anchoring our beliefs to the solid teachings God wants us to know.

It's a guide to use when discovering God in different places. If you begin noticing God in nature, it's a wonderful appendix to see how God created everything around you.

It's a guide to help you discern truth from false teachings. God isn't a God of contradictions, so the Bible gives us a starting line where we can understand God's mind. It's a lesson in God's modus operandi. In other words, much like a mechanic knows how a car moves from point A to point B, the Bible gives Christians the how-tos when it comes to understanding God's mode of operation.

It's a revelation

The bottom line is, the Bible is a revelation from God...to man...about God. As you begin duplicating what you believe with someone else, the Bible is the source where you'll find out who God is and what God's doing throughout history, and you'll be able to infer some transcendental truth as time marches from Moses' day to the present.

Be careful and be on the lookout for false teachers. Some will say, "Every word in the Bible should be taken literally." Just ask them to tell you literally how some 10-headed dragon is going to come out of the sea as pointed out in Revelation. Their answer will be, "Oh, well, that's just symbolic," and then you got 'em. You can't take the Bible 100 percent literally without any reference to symbolism. The Bible contains a mass of symbols and metaphors, and it takes an astute mind to figure out the times when God is telling us something literal versus something metaphorical.

Others will claim, "It's merely a good book with good stories and has nothing to do with the present time." You can ask those naysayers if Jesus was just a story. If not, which parts are just stories? And then you got 'em. We must return to a culture of intelligence. So many Christians just regurgitate a sermon or a book they read *about* the Bible. You must investigate the stories. You must ask questions about the characters. You must be able to lay your own preconceptions at the threshold of truth and allow God to speak through the Bible.

Make sure you read the Bible for yourself. Ask your pastor, youth pastor, or someone you think has a good handle on theology what they think, and then get to know God.

God wants you to know him.

God created you to know him.

The biggest thrill in the fabric of the universe is when people search for and understand God's heart. Then, and only then, does peace really happen. Why? Because you were made for this purpose.

But as quickly as you desire peace and understanding, let me warn you: You must be careful on your journey. No one has the corner on the market of truth. No one completely understands the way to use the Bible. We all understand the basic truths of unity among believers—mainly God, Jesus, his son, and the Spirit of God here to help us understand God in our day.

The Bible is the beginning of your journey.

Read it carefully.

Read it critically.

Read it with a mind's eye to understanding God's heart.

Read it through the lenses of the ancient church mothers and fathers.

Read it through the mind's eye of *your* pastor.

Then you will be spiritually walking to the places God wants you to go.

CHAPTER TWELVE

WHO'S THIS "PERSON" EVERYONE PRAYS TO?

Oh give thanks to the LORD, for he is good;

for his steadfast love endures forever!

—PSALM 118:1 (ESV)

But when we are faithful to keep ourselves
in His holy Presence, and set Him always
before us, this not only hinders our offending
Him, and doing anything that may displease
Him, at least willfully, but it also begets in
us a holy freedom, and if I may so speak, a
familiarity with GOD, wherewith we ask, and
that successfully, the graces we stand in need
of. In fine, by often repeating these acts, they
become habitual, and the presence of GOD

is rendered as it was natural to us. Give Him
thanks, if you please, with me, for His great
goodness towards me, which I can never suf-
ficiently admire, for the many favors He has
done to so miserable a sinner as I am. May
all things praise Him.

—BROTHER LAWRENCE,
PRACTICE THE PRESENCE OF GOD, LETTER 1

C an you imagine what the beginning of time must
have been like? I don't mean the beginning of
school or the beginning of the World Series. I mean
the beginning of the beginning. What was it like? Out
there in the universe, nothing but dark—I wonder how
that felt to God. It must have been a whole lot of nothingness.

No people.

No sound.

No music.

No art.

No nature.

Just nothing.

Was there just vast nothingness in the universe that somehow just exploded?

Did God create all we see as detailed in Genesis?

If so, we have to ask the question, "Who is this God?"

Where did God come from?

What an intriguing thought! Now, some of you are treading on thin ice as you even entertain the idea of creation, but in order for you to own your faith, you must be willing to ask simple questions about God.

Did God have a beginning?

Can it be drawn into a timeline?

Did God have a mom?

Or, has God simply "always been"?

When did we humans first entertain the idea that God is a supernatural Creator, able to do all things on heaven and earth?

Was it from Adam?

Was it from Moses?

I suppose if God just spoke from the clouds, it would be easy, but I've never heard God do that. Maybe I'm not listening, or maybe God just wants me to investigate a little more.

Ancient civilizations gave him attributes like the god of the sea, the god of the sun, or the god of some mountain that gets angry unless there's some sort of sacrifice. Different cultures have adopted different versions of God and formed all sorts of world religions. But, how does the God of the Bible measure up? What is God like? And why should you pray to this particular God?

WHAT MAKES THE BIBLE GOD SO DIFFERENT FROM ANY OTHER "GOD" ON EARTH?

Elijah knew God was different.

He looked all over the countryside and saw people worshiping different gods. The two most popular gods of the day were Baal and Asherah. God appeared to Elijah one day and told him to rebuke King Ahab for his deliberate disobedience in leading Israel away from the one true God, and 1 Kings 18 recounts one of the most amazing stories of all time.

Elijah went to King Ahab and stood in front of him like a scene from one of those old western movies. You know—the ones where the guy in the white hat stands on one side of the street, and the guy in the black hat stands on the other, each of them with an itchy trigger finger to take the other guy out of the world?

Elijah told Ahab to call up the 450 prophets of Baal and the 400 worshipers of Asherah and meet him on top of Mount Carmel. There was going to be a showdown: 950 pagan worshipers versus Elijah. Surely Ahab must have been grinning with glee, knowing he was about to orchestrate the murder of the last faithful prophet to the God Yahweh. As I read the story, I can almost hear him laughing that cheesy black-hat cowboy laugh. "Oh, yeah? Make my day."

Elijah probably just stared him down like Clint Eastwood's character Dirty Harry. But here's the difference between Clint and our friend Elijah—Elijah didn't know why in the world he called them up to Mount Carmel. He didn't know if God was going to consume them all in one bunch or if they would end up torturing him to be a martyr. No, although he was probably serious on the outside, I can imagine him shaking on the inside, full of insecurity, and totally overcome with uncertainty.

I've been standing in Elijah's shoes when I've felt like God has asked me to stand up for something, and I'm not sure how or why.

I've been in the middle of trying to defend God to intelligent people, only to wonder why God put me in this position. Why does God do that kind of stuff?

Because God's different from any other god.

God asked Elijah to gather all the pagan prophets up on Mount Carmel, so Elijah complied like a good prophet would. He didn't know why, but in the heat of the standoff, he shouted out to the pagan guys, "I, even I only, am left a prophet of the LORD, but Baal's prophets are 450 men. Let two bulls be given to us, and let them choose one bull for themselves and cut it in pieces and lay it on the wood, but put no fire to it. And I will prepare the other bull and lay it on the wood and put no fire to it. And you call upon the name of your god, and I will call upon the name of the LORD, and the God who answers by fire, he is God" (1 Kings 18:22-24, ESV).

And I can hear an awkward silence right before Elijah probably thought, *Did I just say that out loud?* And then the people started hunting for a bull.

So they got their bull and called on their god, and you know what happened?

Nothing.

Not a single cloud.

Nothing at all.

Elijah thought he was hot stuff, so he taunted them with a little early prophet trash talk. "Cry aloud, for he is a god. Either he is musing, or he is relieving himself, or he is on a journey, or perhaps he is asleep and must be awakened" (1 Kings 18:27, ESV).

So they started crying louder. The Bible says they started screaming and cutting themselves to try to provoke some sort of response. And all they got was an awkward silence.

Can you see it in your mind's eye? Elijah was probably strutting around, knowing they weren't going to be able to do anything, but then...it was his turn.

Elijah got a bull, placed it on the altar, dug a trench around it, and used 12 stones to represent God's chosen tribes. He thought he'd make it interesting and asked the pagan guys to "'fill four jars with water and pour it on the burnt offering and on the wood.' And then he said, 'Do it a second time.' And they did it a second time. And he said, 'Do it a third time.' And they did it a third time. And the water ran around the altar and filled the trench also with water" (1 Kings 18:33-35, ESV).

Can you believe that? Elijah wasn't content with just asking God to come down and consume a bull while the other god was silent. No, he wanted the thing to be drenched. He wanted to show these guys that God is a God of the impossible. And, so after he made his wet trench with bull pieces on the altar, he prayed.

"O LORD, God of Abraham, Isaac, and Israel, let it be known this day that you are God in Israel, and that I am your servant, and that I have done all these things at your word. Answer me, O LORD, answer me, that this people may know that you, O LORD, are God, and that you have turned their hearts back" (1 Kings 18:36-37, ESV).

I don't know about you, but that's a pretty gutsy move. Elijah must have known something I don't know about God. I mean, I've prayed for things before, and sometimes God doesn't answer. Sometimes it seems like God just leaves me hanging. But not Elijah. Elijah Eastwood just looked them in the eye and said, "Go ahead, make my day."

Just when the sky seemed calm and the prophets began to smirk, the impossible happened.

"Then the fire of the LORD fell and consumed the burnt offering and the wood and the stones and the dust, and licked up the water that was in the trench" (1 Kings 18:38, ESV).

God did it. He showed all the other followers of Baal and Asherah the pagan gods weren't real. In one fell swoop, God consumed the bull—water and all.

The Bible says all the people declared the Lord God of Israel the true God, and the pagans—well, they didn't fare too well. That day, the judgment of God fell on them, and they were all slaughtered. All of them. Together in one realization of God's true power.

So how in the world does this story outline the origin of God or the person we pray to?

God wants us to know he is God

From the beginning of known humanity, God was interested in all humanity knowing he is God.

God made the rules.

God started everything we see.

God was in the beginning before there was even a beginning to begin.

In the Garden of Eden, God communed with Adam.

Before the flood, God told Noah to build the ark.

God led Moses with a pillar of fire by night and a cloud by day.

God gave Abraham a baby son after he was too old to be having kids. God gave a vision to Isaiah and showed a promise to Jeremiah. And God showed up on earth as one of us to help us understand God's unending love for us.

God didn't consume the bull for some cheap trick or a throwaway western movie. No, God allowed Elijah to be on the scene to show Israel those other gods were nothing more than man-made idols. They were destroying their culture, creating a social structure of deviants, and forsaking the fact that he was God.

That's who we pray to. God is a God who is willing to use any means necessary to pull his people back into a loving relationship with himself, and the Bible is full of examples where God shows up and weird, incredible things happen.

We pray to a God who's master over all natural laws, and on God's command, a drenched bull can be consumed by fire from the sky.

God wants us to understand how much he loves us

God loves us so much that God's willing to sacrifice the very physical laws he created in order to help us understand that he is who he says he is.

I must admit, if Elijah had called on God, and God didn't show up, it would have been defeating. Can you imagine?

Of course you can.

You've probably prayed for God to show up in a certain circumstance, and nothing happened. Maybe you called on God to heal somebody you cared about, and God didn't do it. Maybe you asked God to reveal himself to someone so she could go to heaven, too, and God didn't make that appointment. Guess what? Me, too.

I've been so ready for God to work in the lives of some of the teenagers I minister to, and sometimes I feel like they're almost there, and then—well, they end up just going back to their old habits, and I feel like a total failure.

One thing Elijah didn't lack—guts.

He didn't let his insecurities get the best of him. He called on God, and he believed God would do something miraculous. He knew, as he stuck his neck out on the line, God would be there.

He knew, because he knew God.

He knew the character of God.

He spent time understanding and listening to God...

...which is one thing we don't do real well.

It's really a lost discipline in our culture. We spend so much time listening to other things, and then when we try to pack in our God time, which we fail miserably at, we expect God to show up like a genie waiting to grant three wishes. That's not how Elijah did it.

Elijah chased after God because he knew the old stories about how God saved people. He lived through times when there was obvious divine interaction. Elijah gave up everything to understand who God was.

Do you know God like that?

I don't—at least not most of the time. Sometimes I feel like God is all around me and I can do no wrong. Almost like Superman with superhuman powers, I feel like I can walk into any situation and everything will be all right. But then there are the lonely times.

There are definitely times in my life when I feel as if God just turns his head away from me and lets me experience life on my own. Sometimes I wonder if my prayers are just empty words that rise to the ceiling and then vaporize.

But that's not God. The God I know to be true is a God who sits on the throne of heaven and earth and controls all things. The Bible says, "By faith we understand that the universe was created by the word of God, so that what is seen was not made out of things that are visible" (Hebrews 11:3, ESV).

It is God who created.

It is God who maintains.

It is God who offers the reconciliation for the sin in the world today.

God is redemptive.

God is interested in global events.

God is deeply working in the hearts of those in the darkest jungles, and at the same time, God orchestrates the rhythm of the wildest cities. God challenges believers to continue to grow in their knowledge and understanding of him and desires more than anything to have communion with humanity.

HOW DO YOU LEARN MORE ABOUT GOD?

When I was growing up in the church, my parents insisted that my brother and I participate in Sunday school. So I knew the Bible stories backward and forward.

My teachers were usually parents of some student in the class, so we all knew each other from school or maybe family relationships. One thing's for sure: If your teacher is friends with your mom, you don't have a chance of getting away with anything. It's like there's a government spy working overtime to make sure you're doing the right things.

Anyway, when I was in Sunday school, I realized there were a few answers that could get me through any question. I hated when the teacher called on me in front of the class, probably because most of the time,

I had no idea what I was talking about. Until I formulated a genius plan.

For three or four weeks, I started writing down the answers to the questions my teacher asked. Maybe if I could get some of those questions right, I wouldn't look like a total idiot in front of my friends.

When the list was finalized, there were six answers that stuck out. I figured you could ask any question in Sunday school, and I could answer it with:

1. God.

2. Jesus.

3. The Holy Spirit.

4. Read your Bible.

5. Pray.

6. Go to church.

It was a winner every time.

"Andy, who helped Elijah?" she would ask.

"That's an easy one...God." And I winked at my buddies across the table.

"How do you know how to talk to God today?"

"Uh, let me see," I'd say, then reach down to my list. Ah—number 5! "Pray?"

"That's right. You're such a good boy, Andy."

I manipulated my way through Sunday school.

The weirdest thing happened as I grew older. Those six answers I used in Sunday school actually started becoming part of my life. I mean, God is the answer to all the questions. Jesus is the Son of God who takes away the sins of the world. Reading my Bible? Well, that's the way to find out more about this heavenly being called God. The Bible is the way God reveals himself to believers.

But that's not the only way.

Have you ever watched the sun set over the ocean?

Have you ever seen the majestic mountains of Colorado at daybreak? Have you ever stuck your nose over the edge of the Grand Canyon?

Have you ever heard the sounds of the animals in the jungles of Central America?

Have you ever seen a baby sleeping?

Have you ever watched a lightning storm in the desert?

What about a beautiful prairie view just as the sun hits the horizon and all the light turns purple?

God definitely reveals himself in nature.

But that's not the only way.

Have you ever had a meaningful conversation with a friend?

Have you ever laughed with someone so hard that your gut hurt?

Have you ever had someone give you a hug when you thought the world was going to end?

What about a youth pastor or pastor who can speak just the right word at just the right time?

God certainly reveals himself through other people.

But that's not the only way.

Have you ever worshiped God?

I mean truly worshiped with everything inside you?

Have you ever journaled your thoughts?

Have you ever participated in a service with a lot of believers, but sensed God was telling you something specific?

God reveals himself through worship.

God reveals himself in secret.

God reveals himself through corporate service, too.

God doesn't hide behind some obscure moon in the universe. No, that's not God. God wants you to seek him. God desires that you search for him. God is the essence of all the good in the world, and God wants to have a personal relationship with you.

That's the God I know.

WHAT ABOUT THIS JESUS CHARACTER?

Your attitude should be the same as that of Christ Jesus:

Who, being in very nature God, did not consider equality with God something to be grasped,

but made himself nothing, taking the very nature of a servant, being made in human likeness.

And being found in appearance as a man, he humbled himself and became obedient to death—even death on a cross!

Therefore God exalted him to the highest

place and gave him the name that is above

every name,

that at the name of Jesus every knee should

bow, in heaven and on earth and under the

earth, and every tongue confess that Jesus

Christ is Lord, to the glory of God the Father.

—PHILIPPIANS 2:5-11

There is no question—Jesus of Nazareth is the most influential personality in all of humanity. His influence can be seen in most of western civilization, post AD 33. Just look around you. Even today, wonderful works of art are produced with Jesus as the subject, incredible music is composed with Jesus at the heart, and libraries of books analyze his life and teachings from just about every perspective known to man. He has transcended his time period and has become a part of every person's world, whether they believe he is who he said he is or not.

The fact that Jesus walked the earth can't be disputed. Jewish historians such as Josephus document Jesus' travels and sometimes even declare him to be God.

No matter. We're not interested in a history lesson as we begin to document and duplicate what belief is. We're interested in Jesus' heart.

How did he get here?

Why did he come?

And, if we choose to believe he is who he said he is, what's our responsibility to that particular belief today?

At the heart of the Christian faith stands a man, Jesus, the Redeemer of the world. As you share your life journey with your friend, it's vitally important that you not only spend time learning about Jesus, but that you also spend time putting into practice his teachings. Let's examine a few of the latter questions, and we'll try to figure out some practical ways to understand the heart of this man called God.

HOW DID HE GET HERE?

In those days a decree went out from Caesar Augustus that all the world should be registered. This was the first registration when Quirinius was governor of Syria. And all went to be registered, each to his own town. And Joseph also went up from Galilee, from the town of Nazareth, to Judea, to the city of

David, which is called Bethlehem, because he
was of the house and lineage of David, to be
registered with Mary, his betrothed, who was
with child. And while they were there, the time
came for her to give birth. And she gave birth
to her firstborn son and wrapped him in swad-
dling cloths and laid him in a manger, because
there was no place for them in the inn.

—LUKE 2:1-7, ESV

Can you imagine your emotions if an angel came to
you one evening to give a message from God? Never-
mind that he announces you're going to be pregnant
with the child who will save the world from their sins.
No, I'm just talking angelic appearance.

What do you say to an angel? "Uh, hi," seems a
little strange.

"Mr. Angel, sir, can I help you?" seems kind of stupid.

What do you say? How do you act? Do you stand?
Bow? Sit? Lie face-down on the carpet in fear?

The Bible gives an account of the beginning of Jesus' life on planet Earth. It talks about a message from
Gabriel being sent to Jesus' earthly mother Mary. It

records the account of Mary's visit with the heavenly being in detail, and in the middle of the message, he tries to explain how she will carry a child in her untouched womb (Luke 1:35-38).

Talk about an intense encounter! God decided that the redemption of the earth would start with a young woman (likely a teenage girl), who, without any knowledge of sexual relationships, would give birth to the Savior of the world. There are so many Bible stories I would love to have seen firsthand, but Mary's reaction to this heavenly news is up near the top of the list.

The first question I always wonder is, *How did she handle it?* I mean, after she got over the physical shock of Gabriel standing in the living room, what did she say?

If I were in Mary's sandals, would I try to joke around with Gabriel to ease the natural tension and tell him he showed up at the wrong house?

Would I deny the news and in anger go away to pay no attention?

Would I hear Gabriel or just marvel at his angelic characteristics?

Would I be consumed with his presence?

Would I go out and have an abortion to protect my name's sake and the name of my future husband?

After Gabriel told Mary that she was going to conceive the Son of God and that her relative was going to conceive John the Baptist even though she was too old, the Bible says she looked at Gabriel and declared, "Behold, I am the servant of the Lord; let it be to me according to your word" (Luke 1:38, ESV).

Mary was an amazing and extremely important woman. She never claimed to be deity or able to forgive sins, but she was definitely someone special. Mary holds a unique place in history because she gave birth to the Savior, Jesus.

She was the one who was strong enough in the face of all the distractions. She kept Jesus in her womb when her community could have shunned her for what they would have assumed was adultery on the eve of her marriage.

It's easy on this side of life to point at the cute pictures of the nativity each Christmas and watch the peaceful Mary and Joseph look over their little baby, but take a second to put the events into context.

Questions of adultery?

A marriage bed defiled?

Angelic visions?

Savior in the womb?

Mary was a virgin. She shows up at the local Rotary Club meeting pregnant, and her belly starts growing. The other ladies start pointing to her obvious weight gain. "Mary, you need to start dieting." "Hey, Mary, would you like to start walking with me in the morning? We go about three or four miles around the block."

The whispers in the corner alone would drive somebody insane. "Did you see that Mary girl? I can't believe her father lets her out of the house. I wonder what her fiancé thinks about her now."

Surely the rumors were flying when Mary grew to term with her miraculous conception. But God wanted it that way.

We don't know why exactly. Oh, some will try to convince you it's because God didn't want the Son of God to be conceived in an act of primal sexuality, but that doesn't make any sense. If God didn't think sex was a good thing, then why did he create it?

Some try to explain it away as the half-human, half-God scenario. Jesus had to be half genetically God and half genetically man because that's the only way we could have a "real" sacrifice for our earthly sin nature. And that theory seems a little silly, too. If God wanted to impart his power to anyone, certainly it wouldn't matter how the person was conceived, right? I mean, let's remember for a second—God is, well...God, right?

No, I think the reason for Jesus' conception is a great mystery in the Bible. Whatever the reason or the meaning, the bottom line is that God showed his power in it; God fulfilled a promise to send a Messiah through the birth of his son, Jesus. He got here by a grand miracle. There must be something else there; let's ask a few questions.

WHY DID JESUS COME HERE?

Okay, if God is real and Jesus was with God in the beginning (John 1:1), then why did Jesus come to earth in the first place? Surely there was an underlying reason God chose this time in history, in this place, for a specific mission, right?

His mission can be debated until the end of the age. Jesus made it clear in reference to his second coming: "But concerning that day and hour no one knows, not even the angels of heaven, nor the Son, but the Father only" (Matthew 24:36, ESV). So maybe we can infer that his first coming was a mystery as well.

Sure, the Bible contains more than 60 prophecies about the arrival of the Messiah who would take away the sins of the world. He was to come and set up a kingdom where the God-fearers would have no more oppression, no more pain, and no more sorrow. In fact, the Jewish nation was waiting for the day when God would send a final prophet to help them get back to being the ruling nation God promised they would be in the covenant with Abraham.

Isaiah 9:6-7 chronicles the words heard at Jesus' birth that outline his job here on the planet. "The government will rest on his shoulders. And he will be called: Wonderful Counselor, Mighty God, Everlasting Father, and Prince of Peace. His government and its peace will never end. He will rule with fairness and justice from the throne of his ancestor David for all eternity. The passionate commitment of the LORD of Heaven's Armies will make this happen!" (NLT).

The Jewish people expected this leader to come and rescue them from Roman oppression. Jesus' arrival was supposed to introduce a new time of peace and tranquility among the Jews.

But instead of establishing an earthly kingdom, Jesus came here to reconcile all of sinful humanity to God the Father, and in the meantime, he began teaching us how to love one another here on earth.

He came to take away the sins of humanity

The New Testament reveals Jesus' reconciliation mission. Colossians 1:19-20 says, "For in him all the fullness of God was pleased to dwell, and through him to reconcile to himself all things, whether on earth or in heaven, making peace by the blood of his cross" (ESV). Jesus' mission on the planet was to make peace and to restore all of creation to the way God intended it.

When Jesus went to the cross and said, "Father forgive them, they know not what they do" (Luke 23:34, ESV), he was literally appealing to God the Father for forgiveness of a people group lost in the darkness of execution. While he was reconciling their souls to God the Father, Jesus looked down on the soldiers putting him to death and forgave them—just like God the Father looks down on the earth and forgives the people who accept and believe in him.

He came to heal the sick, feed the hungry, and save the lost

Matthew wrote about Jesus' purpose: "And he went throughout all Galilee, teaching in their synagogues and proclaiming the gospel of the kingdom and healing every disease and every affliction among the people" (Matthew 4:23, ESV).

His ministry was filled with miraculous signs and wonders that were otherworldly in origin, starting with the very announcement of his birth. The Bible tells of angels miraculously appearing to shepherd boys in the field, declaring the arrival of this special little one who had come to save the world (Luke 2:8-12).

Don't be fooled. Jesus' mission wasn't only to reconcile man and God. As he healed the blind, fed the hungry, and gave hope to those without any, Jesus started to impart the beauty of heaven to an earth that had long forgotten.

He started reinventing the original intent of creation, as he did away with sickness, cast demons out of men, and helped teach a group of disciples how to live.

When Jesus claimed that the most important part of the gospel was to love God with all your heart and then love your neighbor as yourself, he took the culture of the day and turned it upside down. Up until that point, the term *neighbor* meant a fellow believer, but Jesus had other people in mind.

He longed for a people group who stopped fighting.

He wanted to see an end to bickering, arguing, and self-service.

He began a mission to set servanthood as the highest priority.

As you begin to study Jesus' life, it's amazing to realize there was a lot more to it than the crucifixion and his resurrection. Although they're the most significant points in Jesus' life, the earthly priorities he shared with us can transcend the Hebrew culture and translate into our American culture today.

As you start becoming more like Jesus, ask those you're discipling how they can apply Jesus' life to their own today. It will change the way you live today, tomorrow, and the rest of your life.

THE 33-YEAR-OLD PROPHET

Have you ever taken inventory of life at certain ages?

I do.

I wonder what it was like for my dad to turn 16.

Did he have a nice car?

What was it like when my mother went to college?

Was it too terribly different from my circumstance?

I recently turned 30, the same age Jesus was when he started his earthly ministry with the disciples. What a mind-bender to think that Jesus accomplished all he did between the ages of 30 and 33.

He healed the sick.

He fed the hungry.

He forgave sinners.

And if we're truly honest, he began a revolution the world had never seen.

Jesus had big visions for his life. Of course, he was God, but he was also man.

He worked as a carpenter.

He felt hunger.

He felt pain.

He felt loneliness.

He knew the sadness of losing a friend.

He understood the pain of betrayal, and it hurt his heart.

I think that's why I can identify with Jesus in most areas of my life. I feel all those things, too, and living vicariously through God's humanity frees me. It gives me hope that I'm not alone.

If God came to earth and felt the same things I'm feel-ing, then when I pray, I'm not praying to some ethereal

God. I'm not praying to some God who doesn't understand my circumstances.

I'm praying to a God who can relate to every feeling I'm going through right now. And that's what sets Jesus apart from any other man-made god in the world.

THE SON OF GOD

Jesus knew God the Father. He spent time seeking him. He understood the importance of praying to God because of his past interaction.

Imagine that!

Jesus sat on the throne of heaven before he came to earth. He had the command of legions of angels. He was in the beginning during creation. He walked in heavenly places.

But the Bible says, "While we were still sinners, Christ died for us" (Romans 5:8). Did you catch that? Jesus died for you and me even though he could have called down the angels to save himself.

He didn't have to include Judas in the count of the 12.

He didn't have to answer Pilate.

He was *God*.

He could have looked down at the ridiculous nature of humanity and just declared it a loss, but he didn't. In all his deity, Jesus came to help us be adopted sons of God (Ephesians 1:5).

You know the reason Christianity makes so much sense to me? It almost beckons me to relate. The God on high thought of me so much that he gave his life for my benefit.

Try finding some other religion where its god did anything for you. It doesn't exist.

Christianity is a religion of giving.

It's a place of mercy.

It's a lifestyle centered on forgiveness. And as I walk through life doing those things for other people, Christianity makes more sense.

It's the way the world was designed. For people to be able to forgive others unselfishly is a tremendous law of the universe, and the culmination of perfection happened when Jesus walked the earth.

That's who this guy Jesus is. He's a Savior. He's a Redeemer. He came to show us the real meaning of life, unadulterated with human lusts for worldly things. Jesus makes sense.

IS THE HOLY SPIRIT REALLY A GHOST?

In answer to your inquiry, I consider that the
chief dangers which confront the
coming century will be religion without
the Holy Ghost, Christianity without Christ,
forgiveness without repentance, salvation
without regeneration, politics without God,
and heaven without hell.

**—WILLIAM BOOTH,
FOUNDER AND GENERAL OF THE SALVATION ARMY**

t was just another day—as if any day could rival this
one, given the storm he just calmed. It didn't smell
like a normal storm. The clouds seemed darker. The
rain seemed to come down harder. The wind howled
through the canyon, almost sending the boat to the

bottom of the sea, and all of a sudden, he just calmed the wind and commanded the water to stop churning. It must have been the scariest moment the disciples knew to that point. But in the midst of fear, there was peace. In the middle of the raging storm, there was an unexplainable calm. Something was different about this man.

They felt a new confidence in this man named Jesus, the man who stopped the storms, and they were all poised to witness the next unbelievable miracle from this prophet from Galilee.

Surely they were asking questions. Most definitely they were questioning the validity of this man's source of power to command nature to stop in its tracks (Luke 8:25). Don't you wish you could have been there to witness the disbelief? Do you ever imagine what James and John looked like when Jesus suddenly appeared out in the middle of the lake, on top of the water? What was he doing out there?

Talking to the fish?

Taking a stroll across the curling waves?

Dancing to the heavenly orchestra emphasized by each lightning strike and crash of thunder from the heavens?

They saw him. Peter had his near-drowning experience. They sailed to the nearby beach, and Jesus got off the boat just like every other time. Surreal!

You know, to be honest with you, as I read the Bible, my life has a tendency to seem dull. I think about Jesus' exciting three years with the disciples, and then I look at my life and wonder, *Why doesn't that stuff happen to me today?* My life looks more like the beach they landed on. No welcoming crowds. Just bare desert. Wouldn't it be cool to watch God do something awesome in your life today?

Well, don't just hope for it; look for it. Even though Jesus and the disciples pulled up to a beach seemingly void of anything miraculous, they looked in the distance, and a man came toward them. Eyes darting to the right and left. Hair greasy and unkempt. Clothes tattered. He smelled terrible.

Jesus took one look back at the disciples and then zeroed in on this guy. He had a mission. He started walking away from the boat when the strange man lunged for him. The disciples were a few yards back, but suddenly they hurried to protect their leader from this strange person who certainly called this part of the desert home.

The disciples had heard of this man. In the last town, the people had warned them of a naked vagabond living on the coastline who was banished to the wilderness from the town just a few miles away. His skin was dirty, and his arms were marked with scars from the shackles put on his hands. His feet were bloody from the chains used to keep him locked up and keep the town down the road relatively safe from him.

He wasn't your average hermit seeking asylum from a social system. This guy was strange. It was a spiritual kind of strange. It was the feeling you get when you enter a place that your spirit doesn't quite agree with.

As Jesus approached, the man cried out, "What have you to do with me, Jesus, Son of the Most High God? I beg you, do not torment me" (Luke 8:28, ESV). The disciples looked at each other in confusion. How did this guy know Jesus?

As Jesus walked closer, the man fell to the ground, prostrate, as if to worship or something.

Jesus asked the man, "What is your name?"

The man replied, "Legion."

The disciples backed away slowly. They knew the name Legion. It was a common reference to the demons that would take over a man's body and make him do the most inconceivable actions. The demons had the power to throw the man to the ground and thrash his physical body while tormenting his mind.

All of a sudden, the man's voice changed. It sounded like a monster was inside him. He tried to attack Jesus, but for some reason, he kept getting thrown to the ground. He couldn't get close.

"Jesus. It's not time yet. We beg you; don't throw us into the abyss until the appointed time. Jesus, please, we beg you. Look, the animals near the cliff, let us go to them."

The disciples, still confused, watched Jesus turn. Eyes shut, he looked as if he was praying, and with a quick turn, he faced the man. He held his hands over the man's head and commanded the spirits to leave and enter the pigs grazing by the cliff.

A strong wind blew in the direction of the pigs, and they started to stampede. Squealing and screaming, faster and faster, the disciples watched as the pigs ran straight for the edge of the cliff. A sight that would go down in history, every one of the thousands of swine leapt off the cliff into the sea below to their death.

It happened in less a few than minutes, but the disciples stood, mouths wide open in unbelief. What just happened? How in the world?

Jesus looked back at the man, now calm, and took his cloak to cover the man's nakedness.

"Thank you. Thank you so much. Thank you," the man kept repeating.

"Go and tell the town of all God has done for you," Jesus commanded.

He motioned to the disciples to follow, and they ran to be close to the man claiming to be God.

Can you imagine? Can you see the bewilderment in the faces of the disciples as they wondered how Jesus commanded spirits to leave a human and enter a herd of pigs? Talk about weird! Surely this was one more story they could add to the many times Jesus walked the countryside giving hope to people who seemed to have none.

A CHILDHOOD IN THE DARK

I used to read the Bible as a book of made-up stories. If you think about it very long, it all seems a little weird, right?

A man named Jesus with the power to heal people?

He could make food appear where there was none. He could raise people from the tomb who had been dead for days. It was all a good morale boost, but it never occurred to me that any of those things could actually happen in the real world.

Until I started my own spiritual investigation.

I read Luke 6:17-19 and found Jesus had a special power: "And he came down with them and stood on a level place, with a great crowd of his disciples and a great multitude of people from all Judea and Jerusalem and the seacoast of Tyre and Sidon, who came to hear him and to be healed of their diseases. And those who were troubled with unclean spirits were cured. And the entire crowd sought to touch him, for power came out from him and healed them all" (ESV).

My church never told me about this power. It was all historical lessons to teach me the power of the "God-man"—Jesus. But my church leaders never even thought to ask if these things could happen today, until I started asking questions.

Questions like, "If Jesus could cast out demons and heal disease, could the disciples?" And as I read the Bible, I quickly discovered that the power Jesus used to fight the ills of humanity was made available to the disciples, too.

Luke 9:1 says, "And he called the twelve together and gave them power and authority over all demons and to cure diseases" (ESV). Finally, I found this power wasn't isolated, but was actually revealed and transferred to all 12 disciples as they traveled the countryside.

I still had questions. If this power was given to the disciples, could it also be given to those who believe in Jesus?

Maybe this power could be something to tap into today in this world?

Could it be possible that the authority Jesus had on earth could be given to me today? It makes sense to ask the question. After all, if we don't know if the power exists, then how could we tap into that power? Or, if the power doesn't exist, we could answer the question simply by saying it was only for a time, and now that time is over, and then we could begin pointing out people who are using some sort of power different from God's. It would be a great indicator of what the Bible calls a "false prophet" if indeed the power of God wasn't meant for man today.

WHAT IS THE HOLY SPIRIT'S ROLE IN THE LIFE OF A BELIEVER?

In my own spiritual journey, and in order to become a true follower of Jesus, I found it was necessary not only to obey his commandments, but also to discover the source of God's power as it relates to my own inner struggle.

I had to know if it was possible to overcome sin.

I longed to realize the power of God in my life.

But even up until my college graduation, I was content to know God only through the Scriptures—that is, until I began researching the power of Jesus on my own.

When you read through the Bible, it's clear that the source of Jesus' power came in the form of something he called the "Holy Spirit." When I read Luke 4:17-19, I found the source of Jesus' power when he unrolled the scroll of Isaiah. He declared to the temple leaders, "The Spirit of the Lord is upon me, because he has anointed me to proclaim good news to the poor. He has sent me to proclaim liberty to the captives and recovering of sight to the blind, to set at liberty those who are oppressed, to proclaim the year of the Lord's favor" (ESV).

In Matthew 12:28, Jesus explains, "But if it is by the Spirit of God that I cast out demons, then the kingdom of God has come upon you" (ESV). And he tells his disciples, "The kingdom of heaven is at hand" (Matthew 10:7, ESV).

The kingdom of heaven? Was Jesus trying to tell the disciples there was some sort of supernatural kingdom they needed to accept in order to understand his true message? Even in asking the question, I was opening a can of worms I wasn't sure I wanted to get into. But think about it. If we're going to really become followers of Jesus, isn't it our duty to find out exactly how far God wants us to go in terms of our belief?

I kept reading and found that Jesus said, "And I will ask the Father, and he will give you another Helper, to be with you forever, even the Spirit of truth, whom the world cannot receive, because it neither sees him nor knows him. You know him, for he dwells with you and will be in you" (John 14:16-17, ESV).

In you? What does that mean, the Spirit dwells in you? For my entire spiritual life, I had been told the Holy Spirit was that secret voice in my mind that told me the difference between right and wrong. My Sunday school teachers continually referred to the Holy Spirit as a Counselor who helped me understand the Bible when I read it. But, when I read it, sometimes it didn't make all that much sense. In fact, I questioned the Holy Spirit even being inside me due to the ambiguous stories of the Old Testament.

I needed something tangible. Something more. Where does the Holy Spirit come from? How did he get here? And what difference does the Holy Spirit make in my life today?

HOW DID THE HOLY SPIRIT ARRIVE IN THE WORLD?

Jesus promised the arrival of the Holy Spirit once he was gone (John 14:26). The Holy Spirit was going to help the disciples understand all of Jesus' teachings when he left and be a Counselor to all those who believe in Jesus. But did the Holy Spirit have another job? Is there another reason God put the Holy Spirit in the world today?

Once again, a careful reading of a miraculous story in Acts reveals the origin of the Holy Spirit to believers today.

Luke records Jesus' comments just before his ascension to heaven in Acts 1:7-8: "It is not for you to know times or seasons that the Father has fixed by his own authority. But you will receive power when the Holy Spirit has come upon you, and you will be my witnesses in Jerusalem and in all Judea and Samaria, and to the end of the earth" (ESV).

And that's exactly what happened.

The disciples were hanging out together in the same place when out of nowhere, "suddenly there came from heaven a sound like a mighty rushing wind, and it filled the entire house where they were sitting. And divided tongues as of fire appeared to them and rested on each one of them. And they were all filled with the Holy Spirit and began to speak in other tongues as the

Spirit gave them utterance" (Acts 2:2-4, ESV). This is called the day of Pentecost.

Miracles became the norm instead of something special.

Peter gave a sermon, and 3,000 people believed in Jesus on the spot.

It was the beginning of the global movement we know today as Christianity.

God sent his Spirit to the disciples just as Jesus promised. In all power, all prominence, and all grandeur, God's Spirit came to earth and moved mightily in the hearts of his people.

So the discussion gets complicated when people try to tackle their own understanding of the Holy Spirit.

Is the Holy Spirit still here today?

Is the Holy Spirit still in the business of being the Counselor?

Still in the business of healing disease?

Is the Holy Spirit simply a still, small voice that helps you make difficult decisions and guides you toward understanding God's Word, or does the Holy Spirit move to reveal God's supernatural attributes to man? There are two very different views, and each has merit; and they beg us to continue on a road of discovery.

WHAT CAN THE HOLY SPIRIT DO FOR ME TODAY?

On my journey to imitate, believe, and become a God-fearing Christ follower, it's essential to realize the role of the Holy Spirit in the world today. I've been to conservative churches that teach the "guiding principle," and I've been to Pentecostal churches where people are "slain in the Spirit." Both parties explain their views with valid excerpts of Scripture, but can they both be right? Surely there's some standard we can find in the Bible to help us understand better the role of God on earth.

My journey took me to a small camp in southwest Colorado. I watched God move this particular summer, and it changed my views all together.

I was sitting at my desk when the phone call came through. It was my friend Matthew.

Matthew was a camper at the camp for several years. He kept coming back year after year because he had an experience he couldn't explain. He knew for some reason that God was interested in his life, and he was committed to finding out how to continue his experience throughout the year.

He sounded bothered, distraught, and different.

"Hey, pal, what's up?" I said, trying to break the ice.

"Well, I've got a little problem back here at home."

"What's going on? How can I help?"

"I went to take a physical yesterday, and...well... they found something wrong."

"What do you mean they found something wrong?"

"Andy, they say I have cancer."

My heart sank. It couldn't be true. How could my friend, 17 years old, have cancer? I didn't know much about it, but I was sure I had to do something.

"Matthew, if there's anything I can do..."

The phone was silent on the other end for a moment. "Just pray," he finally answered.

"I'll do whatever I can." My voice strained with distress coupled with anger.

How can God allow something like this to happen? I thought. As we hung up the phone, my heart was heavy with disbelief. I didn't know how or why this kind of thing could happen.

For the next few days I was disoriented in my spirit. I don't know if you've ever felt helpless, like there was nothing you could do, but this was my moment. I felt like I was falling out of control—questioning my spirit, mad at God, not knowing what to do. One night my wife noticed my uneasy feeling, and she asked me pointedly, "Have you even started praying?"

It was the one thing I should have been doing, but for some reason in all the anxiousness, I left God out of the equation. But no more. It was time to get serious about all this.

I rallied the whole camp and explained what was going on in my life, and I asked them to pray. Every day, an hour before our big club-style meeting, I asked them to volunteer to come to the gym and pray for my friend.

The first time we held this "prayer meeting," more than 50 teenagers showed up to pray for my friend. It was so moving. To watch the kids devote their free time to one mission—namely, to praying for my friend—was a surreal experience.

For months we prayed. We prayed for God to move in the physical body of my friend. We prayed for his family to be comforted. We prayed for God's will to be done, whatever it may be.

July 15, the phone rang again. Matthew was on the other end of the line, seemingly distraught again.

"Hey, Andy, thanks so much for all you've done for me. Thanks for your influence. Thanks for the support. Thanks for praying. I went to the doctor today, and they did some tests."

"Matthew, I'm so sorry you're going through this..."

Before I could get everything out, he said, "Wait. They did some tests, and they didn't find any cancer in my body."

"What?"

"That's what I said."

"What do you mean no cancer?"

"They told me I'm fine. Clean bill of health."

"That's awesome," I said, with tears welling up in my eyes. I was so overwhelmed I could hardly stand up.

We finished our conversation, our friendship stronger than ever. Something happened. I'm not sure what. I know my friend was sick, and I know we prayed. I know God answered the prayers of his people in the Bible. I know Matthew didn't go through any formal medical treatment. For some reason, unexplainably, the sickness was gone.

We had a praise celebration that night. The kids who had been praying were excited to see the power of God work through the life of one of their peers. They were excited to see something supernatural, unexplainable, unimaginable happen to a 17-year-old friend.

Now I know God doesn't heal all the time. In fact I know there are prayers every day for the lives of family and friends. I don't know why God heals some and not others. But what I do know—there is mysteriousness about God. God doesn't play by the rules of the earth, and we know that from all the miracles in the Bible.

All I ask is, as you're discovering the power of God in your life, don't rule out the Holy Spirit. Don't rule out the possibility that the Holy Spirit is in the world to counsel, to comfort, and to courageously work the power of God that Jesus promised to the disciples. Check it out for yourself. Ask God to give you a clear picture of the role of the Spirit in your life. And who knows? You might discover something—something radically different from the God you now know.

CHAPTER FIFTEEN

IF I SIN AND DON'T KNOW IT, DOES GOD HATE ME?

For all have sinned and fallen short of the

glory of God.

—ROMANS 3:23

Therefore, if anyone is in Christ, he is a new

creation; the old has gone, the new has come!

—2 CORINTHIANS 5:17

The Garden was perfect. God created the earth with all the goodness in his being. It was the culmination of all his creative energy, and at the end of each day, he declared it good. I assure you, if God says it's good, it's perfect.

On day six, the Bible says, "Then God said, 'Let us make man in our image, after our likeness. And let them have dominion over the fish of the sea and over the birds of the heavens and over the livestock and over all the earth and over every creeping thing that creeps on the earth'" (Genesis 1:26, ESV).

And so God created human beings. It was the beginning of a relationship intended to be pure, righteous, holy, and undefiled. Can you imagine? Man walking with God. Talking with God. Involved in a relationship where there were no secrets, no hidden agenda, and no ulterior motives. Just pure friendship. Pure love from Creator to the created.

He would have done anything for Adam. The Bible says he even noticed Adam's desire for a mate and created Eve. Two beautiful humans. Innocent. Not concerned with work or food or pain. They were the perfect couple living in a perfect world with a perfect Father, God.

And in one imperfect move, it all ended.

God told Adam and Eve, "You may surely eat of every tree of the garden, but of the tree of the knowledge of good and evil you shall not eat, for in the day that you eat of it you shall surely die" (Genesis 2:16-17, ESV).

It was the only rule in the Garden. God set up the earth free from every possible worry, as long as Adam and Eve obeyed the law. Just don't eat the fruit of one tree, or the consequence was death.

That's all it took. Freedom for everything with one restriction, and the two perfect humans focused in on the one tree standing in the middle of all the others. The only one with consequence. The only one that carried the possibility of separation from the perfect world God just created.

Can you see it?

It's like the Christmas gift sitting under the tree left to be opened only on Christmas day. You can play with all the toys you have in the toy room—just stay away from the one box with the wrapping paper on it. I don't know about you, but when I get an order to stay away from something mysterious, I want to find out what's inside. What about you?

For some reason, we have an innate desire to get close to what we're told to stay away from. When one unopened box is kept just within reach, it calls out to the inner parts of your soul to open it. Thoughts string through your head:

No one will know.

It's only one box.

Christmas really isn't that far away.

All it takes is a little encouragement, and then before you know it, wrapping paper is being tossed through the room.

The same thing happened with Adam and Eve. God told them not to eat of one kind of fruit. All they had to do was stay away and obey God's law, but it wasn't enough. It wasn't enough to have access to all the other trees with all the other fruit; no, they had to have the one.

I wonder if they looked at it and wondered. I wonder how many times they passed that specific tree and wondered if they would really die if they ate the fruit.

One day they were walking through the Garden, and the snake appeared to Eve. The Bible says he was craftier than any other animal in the Garden. He looked at the woman and suggested, "You will not surely die. For God knows that when you eat of it your eyes will be opened, and you will be like God, knowing good and evil" (Genesis 3:4-5, ESV). And that was all it took.

Eve looked at the tree, picked the fruit from it, and took the bite that would change the world forever.

WHAT IS SIN?

Sin isn't mysterious.

It's not a mistake.

It's not random happenstance.

No, sin is a definitive action against God's law. The essence of sin is found in a disobedient behavior, thought, or motive that violates God's perfect law.

Sin is actually an archery term. It was used when an archer stepped up to the line to shoot an arrow at a specific target. The goal was for the arrow to travel from the bow to the center of the target. If the arrow hit the center, it was a bullseye. The perfect shot.

If the arrow missed the center and hit any one of the rings around the center, it was a sin. It was, in effect, missing the perfect goal. Missing the mark. And when man misses God's perfect mark—the bullseye for life—it's called "sin."

The consequence of sin started immediately after the action. God takes obedience to his law so seriously that he actually banished Adam and Eve from the perfection of the Garden. He gave them specific consequences they had never even imagined.

He said to Adam, "Because you have listened to the voice of your wife and have eaten of the tree of which I commanded you, 'You shall not eat of it,' cursed is the ground because of you; in pain you shall eat of it all the days of your life; thorns and thistles it shall bring forth for you; and you shall eat the plants of the field. By the sweat of your face you shall eat bread, till you return to the ground, for out of it you were taken; for you are dust, and to dust you shall return" (Genesis 3:17-19, ESV).

One mistake and paradise was lost forever. Man was forced to work, and you might infer that this was the first time man was appointed to die.

To the woman God said, "I will surely multiply your pain in childbearing; in pain you shall bring forth children. Your desire shall be for your husband, and he shall rule over you" (Genesis 3:16). And with one fell swoop, they were sent away—and they were, for the first time, ashamed.

That's how sin works. Even one small, disobedient action and God releases a wave of consequence on the perpetrator. But don't think God wants to sit on the throne of heaven to be the policeman of the universe.

It's not as if God is out looking for people to sin; it's just a fact. A righteous God has no room for unrighteousness in his kingdom. Paul wrote about sin in Romans 3:23: "For all have sinned and fall short of the glory of God."

We're all sinners. We all miss the mark. The consequence of sin is found in Romans 6:23: "For the wages of sin is death." Death! It isn't enough that man is banished from paradise. Now we're destined to die.

It's not as though every time you disobey God, you're going to die, but what would have happened if Adam and Eve hadn't sinned? Maybe we might all be living forever.

The quickest way to be banished from the glory of an almighty God is to disobey, to miss the mark, to sin.

It's a major problem, and God doesn't tread lightly when it comes to disobedience.

WHERE DOES SIN COME FROM?

Jesus told the disciples, "What comes out of a person is what defiles him. For from within, out of the heart of man, come evil thoughts, sexual immorality, theft, murder, adultery, coveting, wickedness, deceit, sensuality, envy, slander, pride, foolishness. All these evil things come from within, and they defile a person" (Mark 7:21-23, ESV).

Evidently sin comes from within humans. Every time you disobey God, the source of your disobedience is within; it's not an external force that makes you do the things God hates.

How can a perfect God create the desires within man's heart that seem to prod him to disobedience?

Why would God allow sin to enter the world in the first place?

How can a good God continue to let sin run rampant when God has the power to annihilate it with a simple thought?

Many libraries carry thousands of books in an effort to reconcile this problem, and the simple fact is, no one knows why.

No one.

No one knows why God continues to allow sin. We only know God does. We only know sin is still a part of the human condition just like it was during Adam and Eve's time. But one thing we do know about the heart of God—at the center of it is the desire to reconcile humanity to himself, so much so that God sent his only son to die a horrific death and be a sacrifice for all the sins of humanity.

As you look at sin and its consequences, it's only natural to ask...

HOW CAN I AVOID IT?

One of the biggest mistakes of 20th-century Christianity is the concept of managing sin. For whatever reason, we have created a long laundry list of sins that are super-important versus sins that aren't so important.

For example, homosexuality will send someone straight to hell while a little "white" lie isn't so bad.

Watching sex in movies is wrong; watching violence in movies is just fine.

It seems that as long as we can avoid the big ones, we can continue to be in fellowship with believers. But, if we cross that fatal taboo list of unforgivable sin, we are destined to a life of loneliness.

Do you really think that's how God sees it?

It only takes a short jaunt to Joshua 7 to see that God takes even the smallest sin extremely seriously.

When Joshua and the Israelites marched around Jericho, God told Joshua not to take anything sacred from the temple. A man named Achan took a little gold and a shiny robe and hid them in his tent.

When the Israelites went to scout out the next land called Ai, a catastrophic even took place. The Israelites were routed, and many men lost their lives.

The people were bewildered. They couldn't understand why God would be with them in certain battles, but in this seemingly small event, God had left.

Joshua fell to his knees and cried out to God, only to find out there was sin in the Israelite camp.

The story is an interesting example of God's righteousness, and Joshua rooted out the problem from the camp. He pulled Achan from among the Israelites and found that he stole precious things belonging to God. He took the things God specifically told them to stay away from.

As soon as Joshua took Achan to the valley, he stoned him in front of the whole nation and then he burned all his possessions. The Bible clearly states that Achan wasn't alone. Joshua didn't just serve this consequence to Achan. He took all of Achan's family, his donkeys, his cattle and his livestock, and all met the same fate on that terrible day.

Then, and only then, did the presence of God return to the nation, and they took the battle of Ai.

The point is, sin is serious. It violates God's law, and God takes his presence away from those who are disobedient. So how do you avoid this loneliness? How can you be sure you don't ostracize God from your world?

The answer is in 2 Corinthians 5:17: "Therefore, if anyone is in Christ, he is a new creation; the old has gone, the new has come!"

Staying away from sin isn't about identifying it and trying to steer clear. The secret to avoiding sin is to stop thinking about your sin and instead, concentrate on your true identity in God.

God didn't say you're a sinner until you die. He didn't say you're a person who struggles with sin as you try to figure out this Christian life. No, he said you're a new creation.

It's like someone who's serious about losing weight. If you want to lose weight and your weakness is ice cream, what's your first thought when you start having hunger cravings? Even more dangerous, what if there's a carton of ice cream in your freezer? How hard is it to continue opening your freezer and look directly at the sweet ice-cream carton? Satisfaction is only a spoonful away.

You're guaranteed to fail.

But what if you think of yourself as someone who just wants to get healthy? You don't diet by trying to stay away from ice cream. You diet by identifying exercise as something good for you. It's a healthy lifestyle. It's a desire to get in shape. You're no longer a person struggling with ice cream; you're a person who desires to simply live healthy. Ice cream tends to fade off your radar screen.

The same principle works with sin. If you wake up every morning as someone who struggles with sin, you're going to continue to struggle. But what if you woke up every morning and realized you're a new creation? What if you woke up every day aware of your adopted status with a heavenly God? You're a new creation! You're not a slave to sin any longer; God made you someone new, as long as you believe in him.

I know it sounds like a simple paradigm shift, but sometimes that's all it takes. A new perspective. A more interesting look at an old problem. You'll never totally defeat sin in your life. You'll always make mistakes. But God says, "If we confess our sins, he is faithful and just and will forgive us our sins and purify us from all unrighteousness" (1 John 10:9).

Isn't that the coolest thing? God wants so much to have a relationship with you that God is willing to forgive you of all your ills, all your wrongs, all your mistakes.

Don't be fooled. Sin is serious. But God is interested in forgiveness.

CHAPTER SIXTEEN

WHY DID JESUS HAVE TO DIE?

> For God has not destined us for wrath, but
> to obtain salvation through our Lord Jesus
> Christ, who died for us so that whether we
> are awake or asleep we might live with him.
>
> —1 THESSALONIANS 5:9-10 (ESV)

The media buzz was intense. I'd never seen the Christian community support a movie like it supported *The Passion of the Christ*. Christians finally had a leader in the engine of the Hollywood machine, and they were putting all their eggs in his basket.

Mel Gibson was a genius creating the movie. He marketed it perfectly. He took rough-cut scenes from his account of Jesus' life and showed them to major Christian leaders around the country. Then after the movie was over, he personally took the microphone and answered questions from the audience. It was awesome. It was like a real-live *Oprah* show. He harnessed our natural desire as a nation to see celebrities, and as he answered individual questions, people really wanted to know about his own spiritual process and the tenets of his faith.

It was certainly the most anticipated movie of all time, at least for the Christian community. Finally, someone was going to tell the true story of Jesus' last week here on planet Earth. We were going to see the nails going into the hands of our Savior. We were going to experience his death in a way our culture communicates—through film.

Churches all over the nation were getting small groups together so people could take their unbelieving friends and pray for a supernatural experience.

I must admit, I was one of them.

I invited my Buddhist friend, thinking if anything could get through to this guy and touch his heart, it would be this explicit, visual story about Jesus.

Boy, was I wrong.

We sat in the movie theater and watched the Roman guards beat Jesus with the long cat o' nine tails. We watched as they put the crown of thorns on his head. We watched as they crucified Jesus.

When the credits started to roll, no one in the theater moved. The lights came on—silence. Nobody got up to leave.

I could hear a few sniffles in the audience as everyone tried to process the brutality of Jesus' death. It was hard to handle, and if you've seen the movie, you know exactly what I mean.

I looked at my friend and asked in a somber tone, "So, what do you think?"

"Let's get out of here. I'll tell you on the way home," he said, trying to hold back the emotion welling up inside.

I thought he must have experienced something cool. Maybe he actually met God here in the middle of the theater.

We walked back to the car, and I was fully anticipating a confession of faith and a long friendship on the Christian journey.

Once again...dead wrong.

"Andy, why are you Christians so violent?"

"What?" I was totally taken aback.

"We would never make a movie and fill theaters around the country to sit in a dark room and watch a guy get brutally murdered. Why? Why do you guys insist on the violence?"

I must admit, I'd never thought of Jesus' death like that. I mean, I always thought of his sacrifice as something good for everyone on earth. John 3:16 says, "For God so loved the world that he gave his one and only

Son." Not, "God so loved the world that he allowed his son to be brutally murdered in the most horrific way known." Even in our present day, there's nothing that compares to the viciousness that accompanies the crucifixion. It's the most horrible death I can imagine.

SO, HOW DOES JESUS' SACRIFICE RELATE TO SALVATION?

The God of the Christian faith is so different from any other god in any other world religion. As I study religions from Islam to Hinduism, no other god sacrifices himself for the sins of humanity. Most of those other gods demand blind obedience for a chance to get to heaven. But the God of the Bible actually came down to earth, out of heaven, and gave his life so you might have salvation (2 Corinthians 5:21).

He came so you can have a more abundant life here on earth (Romans 5:17). He came so you can be reconciled to a holy, righteous God, even though you're a sinner (Colossians 1:20).

The Bible says, "But now he has reconciled you by Christ's physical body through death to present you holy in his sight, without blemish and free from accusation if you continue in your faith, established and firm, not moved from the hope held out in the gospel. This is the gospel that you heard and that has been proclaimed to every creature under heaven, and of which I, Paul, have become a servant" (Colossians 1:22-23).

When we know about sin and the effect sin has on our relationship with God, it beckons us to find an answer. From the beginning of the Jewish faith, God remedied sin with the sacrifice of animals—a blood sacrifice in the temple was required to forgive the sin of humanity.

God's ultimate plan, however, was to send the perfect Lamb of God (1 Peter 1:19) to be sacrificed for the sins of humanity. Jesus was the answer. He was the sacrifice that had to come and begin the restoration of the world to the way God created it. He is God's remedy for a fallen world.

WHAT ARE THE ESSENTIALS IN KNOWING I'M SAVED?

Have you ever wondered *if* you're saved from sin?

Have you ever asked yourself if you'd be in heaven tonight if you died? There are several answers to this question about salvation.

Confess and believe. For sure the Bible says you have to confess. Romans 10:9 says, "If you confess with your mouth, 'Jesus is Lord,' and believe in your heart that God raised him from the dead, you will be saved." But surely confession with your mouth, a verbal "belief," isn't what Paul's talking about.

Think about it. Paul wrote that verse to the Romans who lived under the rule of Caesar. The emperor demanded a confession that Caesar was the lord of all.

The emperors of the day thought they were divine. And anyone challenging their god-like aura was immediately put to death.

Therefore, I don't think Paul just means, "Say a prayer, and you're in the club." He writes to a culture where confession meant your life was in the balance. He was telling the Romans, "It's worth your whole life to confess Jesus is the Son of God."

It's going to cost your life. It's not just a simple confession; it's a death of you—and a rebirth of the new you. Don't get caught up in "American Christianity." We don't know sacrifice. We just want everything to be easy, and real Christianity isn't easy.

Remain in Jesus. Jesus told his disciples, "Remain in me, and I will remain in you. No branch can bear fruit by itself; it must remain in the vine. Neither can you bear fruit unless you remain in me" (John 15:4).

In order to examine your salvation, you must remain in Jesus. It's not like you have to walk around with a crown of thorns on your head or anything. He said, "Remain in me." Later on he says, "If you obey my commands, you will remain in my love" (John 15:10).

That's the hardest part for me. Sometimes I want to live this Christian life on my own. I think I know what's best for me, and when I'm down in the dumps, or when I need God for something, I try to justify my actions and act like I've been faithful in my obedience.

The fact is, I just need to understand what Jesus said—and do it. He has my best interests in mind. And, if you check out his commands under the microscope of experience, you'll find his way works best.

Salvation isn't just some little prayer to say at the conclusion of some Christian meeting. It's more than that.

Take up your cross. "And anyone who does not carry his cross and follow me cannot be my disciple" (Luke 14:27).

Following Jesus is to leave the old you behind, take your life seriously, and follow Jesus unashamedly. It's not comfortable. It's not easy. It's not something that can be wrapped up in a hymn, a worship song, or an after-church potluck. Following Jesus will involve every area of your life and cause you to put the old you to death just like Jesus put sin to death.

He came to the earth from the glory of heaven.

He had angels singing his praises every day.

He walked the streets of gold.

He lived in perfection.

Then he came to earth...

He was born in a smelly feeding trough we call a manger.

He was made fun of and ridiculed.

He walked on the dust of the earth.

He lived amid imperfection.

All so you and I could have a chance at a life of glory. Without Jesus, we are destined for death.

If Jesus gave all that up, don't you think this thing called salvation is going to cost you something?

Take a while to discover the meaning of sin. Don't just take for granted the fact that we all sin, thinking, *That's life;* instead take awhile and work on understanding sin and man's sin nature. It's a wild discovery, and it will help you fully appreciate the grace and forgiveness Jesus came to offer.

CHAPTER SEVENTEEN

IF I DON'T "FEEL" GOD AROUND ME, HAS GOD LEFT ME?

David, wearing a linen ephod, danced before
the LORD with all his might, while he and the
entire house of Israel brought up the
ark of the LORD with shouts and the sound
of trumpets.

—2 SAMUEL 6:14-15

I will not leave you as orphans; I will come to
you. Before long, the world will not see me
anymore, but you will see me. Because I live,
you also will live.

—JOHN 14:18-19

've seen thousands of believers worship God in churches that rival the grandest college football stadiums. The music, the ambiance—it's all like a rock concert drawing believers in the unity of the Spirit.

Songs that call on God's presence fill the halls of our student ministries all over the globe. Worship is an emotional thing. It's a necessary thing.

There's nothing wrong with understanding God with the emotions that well up deep in your soul.

David knew it. David danced before the Lord as the ark was carried from captivity to its home in the temple. Imagine it. Imagine a king—ruling over a nation—defiling the office of kingship because he was so overtaken by the power and emotion of God's grace and forgiveness that he had no other option than to dance in the crowded streets. Can you imagine the president of the United States dancing down Main Street because a religious artifact was being returned to the country after years of oppression? It must have been weird.

When Peter preached his famous sermon in Acts 2, the people thought they were all drunk with wine. But read this: "These men are not drunk, as you suppose. It's only nine in the morning! No, this is what was spoken by the prophet Joel" (Acts 2:15-16).

It doesn't happen every time someone sees God, but it's a fact that when people encounter a living God for the first time, earthly calm passes away, and overwhelming emotion floods the soul.

Maybe you've experienced something like that. When I attended first-grade Vacation Bible School, I read a piece of literature handed out by our leader. It showed the death of Jesus on the cross. It revealed to me the consequences of my sin. And I wept.

When I sit in my church today and the Spirit moves in my soul, I weep. I wonder why a gracious God would send a perfect son to die in my place. The whole experience changes my normal behavior, and I contemplate life without God.

Maybe you know that feeling. You've felt God around you in an unmistakable way. Maybe you've experienced a time in your life when nothing in the real world mattered except the faith you freely received. It's a high like no other, and it should be.

But it fades.

The real world catches us in a web of busyness and focuses our attention on other things. We try to know God's presence, but sometimes it's only a distant memory. I don't know if you've ever felt like that. I have.

So it begs the question, where is he? Where is God when you don't feel evidence of God around? Where are God's loving arms of compassion when you go through a tough time in life? How can you deal with the loss of a loved one in an unexpected death?

Countless teenagers e-mail and ask me, "I felt so close to God one time in my life, but now I don't know what to do. Has God left me?"

HOW DOES GOD WORK IN THE WORLD TODAY?

It's so important for you to understand how God works in the world today, and believe me, I'm not talking as an expert in the area. I'm only trying to describe the way God seems to work in my world.

First, let me assure you, God isn't hiding. God hasn't given up his kingdom for any length of time. And just because you don't feel the emotional presence of God in your life at a particular time doesn't mean God's stopped being God.

God is where God always said he'd be—right beside you. Matthew 28:20 says, "And surely I am with you always, to the very end of the age." Jesus isn't in the business of leaving you. In fact, his desire is for you to remain in him.

So where is Jesus when I don't feel him around?

Ask yourself a few questions, and search this one out on your own. It's not my intention to simply give you easy answers or verses to pass the time. It's my desire that you find the ways God works in the world, and as you share your faith with others, you develop your own story of victory with Jesus.

Think for a minute.

When was the last time God worked in your life?

Where were you?

What things were going on around you that acted as catalysts for you knowing his presence at one particular moment?

There's no magic wand to make God appear, but a careful study of when God showed up in the Bible, who God appeared to, and what the circumstances of God's arrival were may very well lead you back to a place where the presence of God is even more real in your life.

WHY CAN'T I "FEEL" GOD ALL THE TIME?

God is a righteous God. God is holy. God sits on the throne of heaven looking at your life and desiring a deep relationship with you.

The only two things that keep God away are God's decision to stay away and our disobedience. Now, there's nothing you can do about God's decision to remain quiet in your life for a time, but there is a practical way you can deal with your disobedience.

Anytime my students ask me, "Where is God? Why can't I feel him in my life?" the first thing we start to look at is the presence of sin in their lives.

Do you have any malice, deceit, lewdness, anger, sexual immorality, or any other sin oppressing you?

Is there a relationship you need to mend or someone you need to forgive?

Are you serious about your faith?

Do you need to get right with God?

And even then, when you can answer those questions with an affirmation that you're doing everything right, sometimes we just can't explain the lack of God's presence.

It took Job a while to figure out that he was in the middle of a battle between God's word and Satan's conniving actions. It might be, for just a while, that God is proactively being quiet in your life. It may be that there's a bigger plan for you at work.

When the presence of God leaves my life, I always check my sin meter and figure out if I'm justifying some kind of active sin in my life. Next, I return to God's Word and meditate on it. I read Jesus' words and try to let his teachings soak up inside my soul.

And if that doesn't work, sometimes I just go find a worship service close by and try to kneel before Jesus to lay my life at his feet. God is a God of worship. He desires our praise. Sometimes a simple return to those moments of worship can deliver us out of depression and help us see that God is there, ready for our next move.

WHAT SHOULD I LOOK FOR IN MY DAY-TO-DAY LIFE AS I SEEK GOD'S WILL?

One of the simplest ways to see God at work is to pray. When we pray, there's communication with God. We talk. God hears us. Sometimes God answers. Sometimes God's quiet. But in our instant society, sometimes we look for God to behave like a drive-up window attendant at a fast-food restaurant—and we don't allow God to be God.

A few years ago, I started a prayer journal. I started listing the things I prayed for, line by line. Then on the other side of the paper, I listed the answers to my prayers. I dated the times God answered the things I was asking for.

Sometimes the answer came in days.

Sometimes in months.

Sometimes, I've noticed, God hasn't answered at all.

Does that nullify the fact that God is still the God on the throne?

Does it reverse thousands of years of history showing that God is the King of all kings? If God doesn't answer me on my timetable, or if God doesn't answer exactly the way I want him to, it doesn't build any sort of argument for the removal of God in my life.

It's an amazing sight to watch God answer prayers from the ink of my own pen. When I look back at my journal, I instantly return to that point where my soul begins to rejoice. My emotions fall into line. My "feeling" of God returns, and I begin to praise God again.

Maybe it's time for you to take a long, hard look at the moments God has been around, and try to focus your attention on the things God's actively doing in your life today. Maybe it's time for a journal. Maybe not.

Whatever method you choose, I encourage you, as you share God's presence with your friends, don't discount the active participation of God in your life. You never know—God might be doing things you don't recognize, just because you haven't taken the time to look.

CHAPTER EIGHTEEN

DOES PRAYER
REALLY WORK?

Is anyone among you suffering? Let him pray.

Is anyone cheerful? Let him sing praise. Is

anyone among you sick? Let him call for the

elders of the church, and let them pray over

him, anointing him with oil in the name of the

Lord. And the prayer of faith will save the one

who is sick, and the Lord will raise him up.

And if he has committed sins, he will

be forgiven.

—JAMES 5:13-15 (ESV)

H ave you ever found yourself in a moment of prayer
when you thought, *God, I hope you're listening to
this?* I have. Sometimes I wonder if prayer is more
of an activity to make us aware of the things around

us, and less of a necessity to call out to God for some miraculous sign.

I mean, let's be honest—how many times have you prayed for something, and God just doesn't seem to be interested in your request? God doesn't tell you he's waiting. God doesn't seem to indicate that he's in favor of granting your particular request. And furthermore you look like a total idiot as you continue to cry out for something that's never going to happen.

What if prayer was just something to make you feel better in a hard time?

Would that change the nature of your prayer life?

On the other hand, what if God was right when he declared that if you're truly sick, the elders of the church should pray for you and anoint your head with oil? What if...you were healed? Would that prayer take on a deeper, more intense level of commitment? Would you find prayer to be an important part of your life, and instead of painfully trying to fill your day with five or 10 minutes here or there, could you imagine a life longing for more?

The most common question I deal with in terms of praying is, "How do I do it?" It's amazing that the culture of Christianity we've created has left people intimidated to talk with God.

I suppose we should be fearful of God. I suppose we should be ambitious in knowing the right way to pray to a God who created all we see, but prayer is probably the easiest conversation you can have in all your life. And what's cool about prayer? It's God's vehicle to give you power beyond your wildest imagination. Let's explore a few minor issues that relate to prayer.

HOW SHOULD I PRAY?

It's the biggest question when dealing with prayer—*how?*

It's kind of like, how do I talk with a friend of my father?

Do I talk to him like I talk to my friends, or do I have to use language a little more polite to address the grand Creator of the universe?

I've heard all kind of prayers—from, "Daddy, thanks for today," to "Oh, heavenly majesty bestowing the great life-giving force of oxygen in my lungs today, we beseech you to help us in this veritable time of need."

Prayer is just a conversation. When Jesus taught his disciples how to pray, he said, "Pray then like this: 'Our Father in heaven, hallowed be your name. Your kingdom come, your will be done, on earth as it is in heaven. Give us this day our daily bread, and forgive us our debts, as we also have forgiven our debtors. And lead us not into temptation, but deliver us from evil'" (Matthew 6:9-13, ESV).

Okay, so you see some things of importance in there? Go ahead and identify the main points of Jesus' teaching lesson. I'll start with the first one as an example, and then you spend time looking for the tenets Jesus is trying to teach.

1. *Our Father in heaven.* So, that's pretty important. If Jesus used it to set up the whole prayer, I think it's important for us to understand the necessity of identifying God for who he is. He's a Father. He's a unifier in terms of *our* Father. And, he's in heaven. It helps to identify whom you pray to in a world where there are many gods and so many man-made deities to pray to.

Now you try. It will be a great exercise as you go through the Lord's Prayer, and as you find different lessons, be sure to make a note of them so you can teach someone you're discipling.

WHAT SHOULD I PRAY FOR?

When I was in elementary school, my cousin got a Commodore 64 computer for Christmas. It was one of the first personal computers ever—but by today's standards, it was a heap of junk. Still, it was the first touch of technology in the home that would allow for personal computer games. We didn't have Nintendo, PlayStation, or Xbox. No, we had this huge Commodore with like 64 kilobytes of memory. It's really nothing to write home about, but it was the first.

I remember sitting at his desk for hours playing a game called *The Olympics*. It was basically a conglomeration of all the summer game sports into one big program. You could be a track runner, a discus thrower, or a swimmer in the grand Olympic-size pool. Then, the game could calculate how you performed against other players or the computer itself to award you the gold, silver, or bronze medal.

It had every national anthem, so if you represented the United States and won your event, it played the "Star-Spangled Banner" through the sound system. The graphics were awesome compared to the old Atari Pac-Man games, and I thought the idea of having your own computer was incredible!

So naturally, being a God-fearing child, I went home and started fasting and praying for God to give me a computer. Talk about asking God for something you don't really *need*! There are starving orphans in Africa just trying to survive, but here I was asking for a computer.

I didn't know any better, and in our own American culture, we forget about the needs of other people and focus on what we want. And I wanted God to show up and give me something I could play with. (I realize the theological implications of my prayer life now, but give me a break—I was just a kid.)

So I prayed and prayed. I prayed for a computer for Christmas. I prayed my mother would spend the extra cash and there would be a new IBM computer underneath the tree that year. And I didn't tell *any-one*! I didn't tell my mom, my dad, or my brother the nature of my prayers. I wanted this to be between me and God. It was almost like I was testing to see if God really listened.

Christmas day soon came around, and I was full of faith, believing it was going to happen. I proudly put on my pajamas and walked down the hall to the area where the Christmas tree stood, and lo and behold, there was a large package that looked like it might be...

My mom and dad joined me in the living room, and my brother started ripping the wrapping paper off every package with a nametag that included even the first letter of his name. He was blowing and going while I stood by, just waiting for my miracle gift to be presented to me.

Sure enough, when my mother asked me to open the big box in the middle of the room, guess what? It was a bicycle.

A bicycle? What in the world? I thought God was going to answer my prayers. I thought God was interested in showing me how miraculous he could be. How in the world was I supposed to trust in a God who didn't answer me? A bicycle is definitely not a computer!

Well, as you can see, being young in my faith, it was only natural to combine the idea of the lack of a computer on Christmas to a lack of faith in God answering prayers.

Does God answer prayers for computers? *Yes!*

Does God answer prayers for test answers to appear in your brain? *Yes!*

Does God heal the sick through prayer? *Yes!*

Does God help you find the right mate? *Yes!*

Does God help you find a job, or a school, or a new vocation? *Yes!*

God is in the business of answering prayers, but sometimes we need to look through God's eyes and try to understand why God does or doesn't answer a particular request.

One thing God is not—a genie. If you think praying to God is like asking the genie in the lamp for three sacred wishes, you've got God all wrong. Prayer isn't about granting you comfort. Prayer isn't about giving you things. Prayer isn't about a self-centered accumulation of a lifestyle free from suffering. That's just not biblical.

What we do know is, prayer is communication with God. We know God wants us to pray a lot: "Pray without ceasing, give thanks in all circumstances; for this is the will of God in Christ Jesus for you" (1 Thessalonians 5:17-18, ESV).

God is interested in your prayers of thanksgiving. He's interested in your attitude in prayer. In fact, Jesus even references a style and attitude of prayer that the Pharisees were adopting when he walked the earth.

He looked straight at the Pharisees when he was preaching the Sermon on the Mount and said, "And when you pray, you must not be like the hypocrites. For they love to stand and pray in the synagogues and at the street corners, that they may be seen by others. Truly, I say to you, they have received their reward. But when you pray, go into your room and shut the door and pray to your Father who is in secret. And your Father who sees in secret will reward you. And when you pray, do not heap up empty phrases as the Gentiles do, for they think that they will be heard for their many words. Do not be like them, for your Father knows what you need before you ask him" (Matthew 6:5-8).

Prayer isn't a show. It isn't a game. It isn't something that makes you more spiritual to God if people think you're a prayer warrior.

Prayer is your communication line with God.

Jesus did it.

The disciples did it.

Paul did it.

It's one of those spiritual disciplines that will take you to a closer relationship with him.

HOW CAN I KNOW GOD IS WORKING THROUGH MY PRAYER LIFE?

Test it. I know there aren't a lot of people out there advocating the quantifying nature of God, but just try it. Remember that journal I wrote about in the last chapter? Take a second to grab a notebook and start by making two columns.

The first column is for requests, while the second is for answers. Go ahead and date the request, and when you sense it has been answered, date the answers. See what happens.

You never know—you just might meet God on a different level, and as you strengthen your faith, you'll have a greater ability to ask God for bigger things.

I don't know about you, but I want to ask God for the impossible, so I can worship God for deliverance in my life. Don't you?

WHY DO I NEED TO READ MY BIBLE?

(I MEAN, WEREN'T THERE GENERATIONS LONG AGO THAT DIDN'T EVEN *HAVE* BIBLES TO READ?)

I have stored up your word in my heart that I

might not sin against you.

—PSALM 119:11 (ESV)

Have you ever picked up your Bible and read some obscure passage that didn't make any sense? I have.

Some of us think we can flip open the Bible to just the right passage, and God is going to mysteriously tell us something about the day. It's almost as reliable as sitting with one of those tarot-card readers flipping the cards around. And, if for some reason you haven't experienced this exercise of chance, try it.

Pick up your Bible, and at random pick out a page in the middle. Put your finger right in the middle. Open it up. And...okay, I opened Obadiah 1:1. "Thus says the Lord GOD concerning Edom: We have heard a report from the LORD, and a messenger has been sent among the nations: 'Rise up! Let us rise against her for battle!'" (ESV).

What in the world does that mean?

How am I supposed to apply that to my life?

Why should I read a book more than 2,000 years old that sounds like some ancient manuscript having nothing to do with my life?

Well, that's where we need a good lesson in understanding the role of Scripture.

You must understand that the Bible wasn't written yesterday. It's not a book that needs any more scrutiny, because man has tried to disprove the Bible ever since it was written.

The historical evidence of the Bible being handed down generation after generation is conclusive. What you hold in your hand is the same book that the ancient church fathers held in their hands—only yours is in English.

So, if the Bible you have is the same as the ones they had, how are you supposed to view reading the Bible?

Many Christian leaders say reading your Bible is the only way you can have a relationship with God. Like I've said before in this book, reading the Bible, quiet times, Scripture meditation—they're all important.

But remember, if you just read the Bible for the words on the page, you've missed the point. It's not some rote exercise you can check off today's spiritual to-do list.

You're not going to accumulate enough Bible-reading time to prove your faith to anyone, especially to yourself—and more importantly, God doesn't care as much as you think. (Okay, for those of you who've just fainted, breathe easy. I promise I'll bring this around.)

So, I propose a new paradigm. Take a step back. Take a second to see the reason why it's important to read the Bible—not so much how you interpret Obadiah or whatever verse you landed on.

THE BIBLE HELPS US UNDERSTAND WHO GOD IS

Remember the chapter about the importance of the Bible? The Scriptures are a unifying document to draw every believer under a specific umbrella of who God is. There are many false teachers, and many who've claimed they're the true God, but in fact, there can be only one God. If there are more, then the one we worship is merely a part of a group, not really the all-knowing, supreme authority we think God is.

So the Bible allows you to read the history of God and his relationship with humanity since the beginning of creation. It gives us a clear picture of God's character. It helps us understand God's specific nuances. It helps us in our journey to know who God is by revealing certain characteristics of God's nature.

Obadiah 1 might not immediately jump off the page, but if you take the time to understand the history, the context, and the way God was working in the lives of the Israelites at that particular period of time, it unlocks another mystery of the Creator God.

Apart from the lion's den and Shadrach, Meshach, and Abednego, the book of Daniel may not be super exciting, either. But if you take a little time to research what God was trying to do in the lives of the young Hebrew men at that time, you can apply what you've learned to your own life. It might give you a little hope when situations seem hopeless. It may, in fact, strengthen your faith to know that in impossible situations, God is still there.

Reading the Bible is an important way for you to discover the core nature of the one who created you.

THE BIBLE HELPS US HEAR FROM GOD IN OUR SOULS

One of the coolest parts of reading the Bible is the way the Holy Spirit speaks to our souls. Jesus says in John 14:26, "But the Helper, the Holy Spirit, whom the Father will send in my name, he will teach you all things and bring to your remembrance all that I have said to you" (ESV).

I recently had a friend text me with a question. "Hey, I just broke up with my girlfriend. Do you have any good verses? Because my heart is hurting."

Okay, the Bible isn't a spiritual antibiotic. You can't just flip it open and have all the pain in life just fade into distant memory; but there are times when the Bible can speak volumes to your heart as it navigates the hurts of life. It encourages your heart through fun times. It gives us foundational precepts to ground every decision we make. God can speak through the Bible.

In Old Testament times, God spoke audibly to the leaders of the Jewish nation, but today, as far as my experience tells me, God speaks through different means—through fellow believers, circumstances, experience. But God also speaks through the Bible.

In the Bible, God speaks through the history of the Jewish culture and the testimony of his son, Jesus. God also speaks through prophecy, poetry, and divine revelation. But don't miss the fact that the Creator of the universe can speak to your soul, whether it's through other means or the Bible itself.

THE BIBLE IS THE STANDARD OF TRUTH

The New Testament says, "Beloved, do not believe every spirit, but test the spirits to see whether they are from God, for many false prophets have gone out into the world. By this you know the Spirit of God: every spirit that confesses that Jesus Christ has come in the flesh is from God, and every spirit that does not confess Jesus is not from God. This is the spirit of the antichrist, which you heard was coming and now is in the world already" (1 John 4:1-3, ESV).

The only way we can test and approve if something is from God is to have a standard.

In the old days, construction workers invented a tool called a plumb line. A plumb line is a string with a small metal weight at the end. The idea behind the plumb line is, if you want to find something that's level, you hold the string at the top of the structure, and the metal ball on the end pulls the string straight down. The angle of the string is supposed to be perpendicular to the ground.

It's the standard by which you can build something that stands straight vertical from the ground. If you line up your walls with the help and direction of a plumb line, the walls will be straight. If you don't use the plumb line, you risk the chance of your walls leaning to one side or another.

The Bible is the same way. If we continue to refer to a plumb line in our spiritual lives (i.e., the Bible), then we'll always be building them knowing there's a standard to measure and test ideas. That's one of the most awesome uses of the Bible. It's a standard by which you can test ideas, beliefs, or any kind of teachings.

If you find the Bible to be boring, or unreadable, or irrelevant in your life, don't give up. Make sure you give it the chance it deserves. It's the only document inspired by the Creator of the universe. Give it a try.

CHAPTER TWENTY

MY CHURCH IS *SO* BORING! DO I HAVE TO GO?

And they devoted themselves to the apostles'
teaching and fellowship, to the breaking of
bread and the prayers. And awe came upon
every soul, and many wonders and signs
were being done through the apostles. And
all who believed were together and had all
things in common.

—ACTS 2:42-44 (ESV)

I hated practice. And the only thing worse than a meaningless practice was a meaningless meeting meant to help us bond. Now, don't get me wrong—I'm the first one to stand up and say I love to hang out. But my coach started forcing this "team bonding" idea, and I couldn't stand it. *Let's just get to the game*, I would think. *Please, I don't need to run anymore. I'm in shape,* I cried out inwardly more than once.

It wasn't that I didn't like the guys or that I disliked basketball, but I found myself sitting in the front of the bus just waiting to get back to my house and my girlfriend. Just to go and hang out for no reason seemed like a waste of time to me.

The same thing happens sometimes when we go to church. Today I understand what my coach was trying to do. He was attempting to put the team in places where we could make memories. He wanted us to live together, eat together, weep together, and rejoice together. For some reason, experiencing life together is often a good thing.

Sometimes at church we ask similar questions. *Why? Why do I have to go be with people I don't know? Why do we have to pray together? Why?*

It's important to establish a purpose for attending church. And believe me, it's not to impress God.

God doesn't care if you merely walk through the doors of a building.

God's not taking roll.

God doesn't care if you sit in the same old seat Sunday after Sunday.

I mean, do you really think God only accepts worship if there's a sanctuary, a baptismal, or a preacher around? Of course not. God isn't bound by a building or a meeting. But God has set up the church for a reason.

THE FELLOWSHIP OF BELIEVERS

The beginning of the church was an eye-opening event. Acts 2 recounts a strange introduction of the Holy Sprit, and when Peter started preaching, the Bible recounts that 3,000 people started following Jesus. It was an amazing beginning, but that's just it. It was the beginning.

It was the beginning of something so special and so pure. The people cared about each other so much that they started sharing everything. The Bible says, "All the believers were together and had everything in common. Selling their possessions and goods, they gave to anyone as he had need" (Acts 2:44-45). Now that's an exciting church.

Can you imagine a place where everybody cared so much about everybody else that they'd all be willing to sell *everything* for someone in need? It wouldn't be about who looked the best. It wouldn't be about who sang the best, who had the most stuff, or even who attended church services the most. The church in Acts was about serving each other. They had pure fellowship.

Unfortunately, most churches are filled with attendees and nothing more. And, as I pointed out earlier, people are sinners. Even in church, the pews are filled with sinners who sometimes don't understand the essence of the meeting.

We gather to praise. We gather to learn. But we also gather to fellowship with like-minded people. When Acts refers to the people as having everything in common, it's talking about people who loved God so much that they were willing to put their own economic lives on the line for each other. That's the way church is supposed to be.

There are no perfect churches, because there are no perfect people. But in order for you to grow in a community of believers, it's worth checking out a church that will allow you to make friends and share life together.

I love the motto of my church here in Missouri. The church constantly focuses on the phrase, "living life together." That's what church is all about. It's not a country club where we can isolate ourselves from the world and give each other knowing winks as if we belong to something special. No, church is about having time to grow together and share our spiritual journeys as we learn more about God.

THE IMPORTANCE OF LEARNING TRUTH

It's so important that you have an outlet that will teach the truth. Church is supposed to be a sanctuary, a place where you can get away from the daily grind of the world and focus on Jesus. It's not a place to have another pizza party at youth group, although I love having fun together. But when you're looking for a place to call a church home, be sure you choose a church to attend where the people are excited about learning foundational truth and living life together.

Make sure the pastor challenges you to grow in your walk with Jesus. Make sure the small-group leaders are well-equipped to help you grow and learn more about this enormous concept, Christianity.

Be sure you don't just go to a church because you've always gone there. If the leadership of the church isn't offering a fertile ground for fellowship with other believers or isn't teaching you how to grow, then pick another one.

There's no perfect house of God, but you can't use that as an excuse to walk away from the fellowship of believers.

You might be thinking, *Well, my church will never be like that.*

You know what? I've heard Christians complain about their churches for a long time about a lot of things.

They complain about the order of service.

They complain about the message.

They complain about the flowers at the podium.

They complain about the old lady in the fellowship hall who runs it like a prison ward.

Just remember, if you don't like it, you have two options. Either leave and find another church or be the beginning of change. Be a leader who can direct your church toward a more "Acts"-like fellowship. Be someone who craves to know more. Be a church member who pushes the pastor to excellence.

I guarantee the pastor at your church doesn't want to babysit a bunch of complainers. That's not why your pastor got involved in ministry. More than likely, the pastor of the old-time dead church has simply been lulled to sleep because the people in the church show no interest.

Ask your pastor hard questions. Show the leader of your flock you're interested in what's going on in the church. You never know—you could be the catalyst in a revolution that would wake up a church on its last leg.

HOW TO SERVE LIKE JESUS SERVED

One of my friends told me the other day, "We never change our behavior until we're forced into positions of change. We're creatures of habit, and unless it's necessary to move, we'll just stay where we are."

It's totally true.

If you want to see a church serving like Jesus served, then you need to start doing it.

How?

Read the Gospel accounts of how Jesus served the people he came in contact with. Jesus was always perceptive enough to notice a physical need, and then he met it.

When he saw the blind man, he noticed it and healed him.

When he saw the people hungry, he noticed it and fed them.

When he saw the demon-possessed man, he noticed it and cast the demon out.

Only after Jesus met a physical need was he given the platform to proclaim truth.

If you want to see a church changed, be willing to get dirt under your fingernails and serve people. If your church needs a small-group leader, step up and volunteer. If your church needs people to greet at the door, then stand at the door one Sunday and, with a smile on your face, welcome people to God's house.

Once you take some initiative, watch people follow you. This isn't rocket science. Just meet needs. God will either change the church, or God might just call you to go to another church where you can be most effective with the gifts God gave you.

Church is not a place where people should be falling asleep. We've turned church culture into "entertain me."

Don't you think Jesus established the church to be an active, organic, living, breathing organism that can only be fed by the energy its members put in it? Take a lesson from Jesus and serve. You'll be surprised at the new ways you'll think about an old boring meeting.

As you explore church with your duplication partner, come up with some ideas to help serve your church. Don't make your spiritual journey just about you two, because if that's the case, you'll defeat the whole purpose. You must be involved in a church. You must be plugged into a community of like-minded believers. It's the next discipline that will thrust you into becoming a disciple who not only imitates, but becomes a follower of Jesus.

HOW AM I SUPPOSED TO LOVE OTHERS LIKE I LOVE MYSELF?

Jesus replied: "'Love the Lord your God with
all your heart and with all your soul and with
all your mind.' This is the first and greatest
commandment. And the second is like it:
'Love your neighbor as yourself.'"

—MATTHEW 22:37-39

It was a hot day in Tempe, Arizona, one of the greatest cities in the country. My friend and I were walking down the famous Mill Avenue when he saw an Urban Outfitters store. "Hey, we need to check that out," he said.

I agreed, and we crossed the street right in the middle of the traffic.

When we got to the other side, I noticed a group of people sitting on the sidewalk outside the store. They weren't your "normal" shoppers, as evidenced by their hippie-style clothes, the brown paper bags sitting beside them, and the hemp necklaces one of the girls was tying.

I told my friend I was just going to wait outside and try to get a conversation started to see what these people were all about. He agreed, so I sat down on the concrete sidewalk next to the necklace girl.

"Hey, those are really cool."

"Thanks. I'm way into weaving these cool stones in the middle of the necklaces. What do you think?" she said as she raised one of her prize creations for me to comment on.

"That's awesome. I've never seen anything quite like that."

"Well, I trade for unusual beads so I can make something no one has ever seen before."

"Do you sell these things? Cause if you don't, you definitely need to open a little shop. This is awesome!"

"No, man. I'm not into selling. It's the law of karma. You just give away what you can, and it will come back to you," she said, like she'd been smoking pot for most of the morning.

I knew I was on to something here.

"So, you just, like, give this stuff away?" I asked.

"No. No. I ask for a donation, but there's no set price. You want one?"

I couldn't believe this girl. Here she sat, obviously living on the donations of people walking by, weaving hemp necklaces in the middle of one of the richest cities in the world. I started wondering, *How is she making it?*

"Hey, is this your only job?" I asked to kind of probe around a little.

"Yeah. We just sit out here every day when the weather's good. If it gets too hot, we just go over there to the railroad and jump the trains that pass by. It's a great way to see the country, and if you feel good about a city, you just jump off and try to figure out where you landed."

"Are you kidding me? You're a real-life hobo?"

"Well, I wouldn't call it that. But, yeah, if we were living in the '50s, you might call me a hobo. I've never really thought about it like that."

"Do you ever run into sketchy people on the train?" I asked. Coming from a suburban upbringing, I always thought it was a little dangerous to just jump a train and travel across the country. "Isn't jumping trains illegal? Isn't it dangerous?"

"No, not really. You know, there's a community of people that just travels from city to city. You run into all kinds of people, but if you just mind your own business, they're all pretty cool."

"Are you serious, or are you just pulling my leg?"

"No, man. I'm totally serious. It's a great thrill to wake up somewhere you didn't plan on being the day before."

The conversation was winding down, and I knew I was going to have to buy something from this girl.

"You know, man, the only people we've ever run into that cause any problems are those Christian people down here."

"What?" I acted like I didn't hear her and tried to renew my cover, as I was obviously one of those Christian people, and I didn't want to get beat up by a girl tough enough to jump trains.

"Yeah. Those Christians, we hate them. They just walk by and try to get us to pray a prayer or something, and then if we don't, they just walk on by. You know, they don't care about us. I mean, how can you care about somebody's soul one minute, and then not care about it at all the next? At least the Jehovah's Witnesses lady brings me cake."

And right then, at that moment, I was ashamed. I was ashamed to be a Christian. I was embarrassed that the name I claimed had such a bad reputation with someone who needed to know God in a real way.

That's what many in the world think of Christians, unfortunately. We're a bunch of snobby people who think we have the answer to all of life's problems. We go around trying to rescue people's souls, but we really find it hard to have long-term, meaningful relationships with anyone.

WE'RE COMMANDED TO LOVE OTHERS

Thankfully, Jesus didn't just walk by. He didn't see me in my sin, hanging down on the corner of life's road, and just walk by. He stopped. He revealed himself to me, and he wants to continue growing me and filling me with his knowledge in all wisdom and understanding.

Loving others is the second greatest commandment, and it's high time we try to figure it out. We have to stop seeing the world as a pity case. People don't want to be rescued; they just want a friend. Non-Christians are no different from you or me, except for one giant fact: You had the opportunity placed in front of you to accept God's love, and you took it; they haven't yet—or maybe they've never had the opportunity.

Don't get caught up in self-serving religion. It's not pretty, and Jesus didn't do it. Jesus sat with sinners. He dined with tax collectors. He hung out with prostitutes. He met the needs of the sick. And he wasn't afraid to confront sin in a loving way.

Just before I left my meeting with my friend in Arizona, I emptied my pockets of all the cash inside. I ended up giving her like $60, and I said, "Hey, Dawn, just so you know, not all Christians act like that." And I walked away. No four-point sermon. No prayer. No argument. No pity money. No, I just tried to give something to someone who had a need.

It's our duty to serve people, whether they're Christians or not. Jesus didn't say to love our Christian neighbors. He commanded us to reach out to all people groups and try to make a difference.

AM I SERVING OTHERS?

If you have to ask the question, then you're probably not. Serving others simply means to see a need in someone's life and meet it.

Homeless people need a home.

Sick people need medicine.

Homosexual people need friends, too.

Drug addicts need a rock of a friend to help them out of addiction.

Elderly people need a smile from a young face.

Christians who publicly mess up their lives need other Christians to forgive them.

If you're not actively searching for a place to serve in your life, then you're missing the heart of the faith. God didn't command you to start another Bible study.

God didn't envision all these Christian small groups forming in order to isolate themselves from the world.

Jesus said to love God, and then go and love your neighbor. It's the heart of the Christian faith.

When selecting his disciples, Jesus said, "Come and follow me." But when it was time for them to go out on their own, he said, "Go." Go and share with them the love I have shown you.

Don't be afraid. God is with you. God will stand by you. Matthew 28 says Jesus will be with you to the end of the age.

Find someone in your community who needs a friend, and start acting like a real Christian. Don't let Jesus' reputation get caught in some salvation discussion where you're not focusing on the person you're talking to. God knows when people are ready, and you don't have the power to save anyone. Just take some time. Be a friend. Meet the needs of those around you, and you'll learn how to truly love. Then at least the door is open for them to see God's love at work in you.

HOW DO I LEARN WHAT "GOOD FRUIT" IS?

Jesus said, "You did not choose me, but I chose you and appointed you to go and bear fruit—fruit that will last. Then the Father will give you whatever you ask in my name. This is my command: Love each other" (John 15:16-17).

He told the disciples to go and bear fruit, and by their fruit he could tell whether or not they really believed.

The idea of fruit is simple. If you plant an orange tree in the right kind of soil, with plenty of water and plenty of nutrients, it has no other option than to produce oranges. It's not rocket science. It just does.

It never produces nuts. It won't produce other kinds of fruit. An orange tree is designed to produce oranges. That's its job!

Christianity is the same way.

If you're grounded in God's Word...

If you're being filled with new knowledge and understanding...

If you're learning the true principles behind Jesus' teachings...

You have no other option than to bear fruit. There will be people in your life, or circumstances you can identify, or experiences you can tell others, that identify you as someone who's living life differently. Others will know you're a Christian. Jesus said, "By this all men will know that you are my disciples, if you love one another" (John 13:35).

If you're a true disciple of Jesus, you will love others. If you find you don't love people, you need to re-examine the soil you're planted in. Maybe you need to check the water you're drinking. Or maybe you need to take a step back and re-evaluate your walk with Jesus.

Just like an orange tree, you don't have to work at it. It just happens out of the design God masterfully made you to be.

Make sure you take some time to discuss this concept with your duplication partner. Part of realizing that you're becoming a follower of Jesus is exploring what others see in your daily life. It's easy to justify behavior, especially when we think we've got the truth. Ask your friend, "What do people think about me? Do you think they see fruit from my relationship with God?"

If not, it could really help you identify areas in your life that need a little work.

Don't be afraid to let someone speak to your soul. Sometimes we live in the "nice" Christian world, and we really need someone to tell us the reality of life. Let them. It may sting at first, but in the long run, you'll be able to adjust your spiritual life according to how you want it.

CHAPTER TWENTY-TWO

OKAY, LOVING OTHERS IS ONE THING...BUT LOVING MY ENEMIES?

But I tell you: Love your enemies and pray
for those who persecute you, that you may
be sons of your Father in heaven. He causes
his sun to rise on the evil and the good, and
sends rain on the righteous and the unrigh-
teous. If you love those who love you, what
reward will you get? Are not even the tax
collectors doing that? And if you greet only
your brothers, what are you doing more than
others? Do not even pagans do that?
Be perfect, therefore, as your heavenly
Father is perfect.

—MATTHEW 5:44-48

After September 11, the whole nation mourned for the shocking, enormous loss of life. America had never been attacked by an enemy like this. We were secure here. With oceans on the east and west coasts, we were protected, right?

I'll never forget watching the planes hit the World Trade Center towers and the Pentagon in flames. I was standing in my living room cradling my three-month-old girl in my arms, and my four-year-old son was tugging at my leg. "Daddy, why is that building burning?"

Through the tears, fears, and the realization the world was changing, I told him, "Son, don't ever forget this day. Someone has done something really bad, and there are a lot of mommies and daddies who aren't going to make it home tonight."

After the media announced that al-Qaeda was the chief party responsible for the bombing, America united like never before in my lifetime. We united under a patriotic spirit. We united to help those who lost so much. We united because that's what we do when things get hard—we pull together and support each other.

For several nights after that terrible Tuesday, I had a nightmare. I was walking down the busy streets of Manhattan, and there in the crowd, he was walking slowly toward me, people hiding him as he moved side to side. His eyes were filled with hate. The crowd parted, and I angrily stood face to face with the biggest enemy I could imagine: Osama bin Laden.

Then I woke up. Every time sweating more than the time before. Every time confused.

It was the weirdest dream cycle, because I rarely remember my dreams. My wife will ask me in the morning if I dreamed, and I can't ever remember if I did or not. It was the strangest thing.

But this dream was clear as day. It was almost as if it was so real, I was beginning to believe it. *Maybe God's trying to tell me something,* I thought to myself. *Maybe I'm supposed to join the army and do something?*

The Sunday after the attacks, the church was full. People came from all over to pray for the losses of those victimized in the attacks. We even had a hard time finding a seat because the sanctuary was so full.

Our pastor called for prayer several times during the service, and when he started the sermon, I almost lost it.

"Who do you hate?" he asked in a melancholy tone. "Is there an individual somewhere in the world who's the object of all your hate?"

Of course I couldn't stand up, raise my hand, and admit my disturbed dream about murdering bin Laden. This was church, right? We don't do that stuff. I almost leaned over to the guy sitting next to me to reveal my problem, but I thought there were only two options for the outcome of my confession. Either he would prop me up, and I would receive a roaring standing ovation for being such a patriot, or I'd be committed to a mental institution.

My pastor wasn't looking for a small army. He wasn't trying to recruit for the Special Forces unit. He was trying to reveal Jesus' heart to us.

"We need to pray for bin Laden today."

What?! Are you kidding me?

Pray for the animal?

Pray for the perpetrator?

Pray for the murderer?

No way.

"God loves him, too." My pastor took a long pause.

I thought, *Well, I don't.*

I don't want to love him.

I don't want to forgive him.

I'm sure you've had people in your life who make you angry. I'm certain there are situations where you can readily identify enemies.

JESUS' TEACHING ABOUT LOVING OUR ENEMIES

Jesus didn't single out good people to be the sole objects of our affection and love. He didn't say, "Go out and love all the people who do good to you." In fact, he said just the opposite. Jesus said, "But I tell you: Love your enemies and pray for those who persecute you, that you may be sons of your Father in heaven" (Matthew 5:44-45).

I'm telling you, I struggled with that. And I guess if I'm honest with myself, I still struggle with loving people who have no intention of loving me.

But Jesus made it clear—I'm supposed to love people. I need to love the bully. I need to love the guy who doesn't pay his bills. I need to love the girl who hates me. I need to love the hobo down in Tempe, even though she hates Christians. I need to love Republicans. I need to love Democrats. I need to love those who are totally irresponsible. I need to love people who hurt my feelings and make me feel unimportant.

In order to be a son of God the Father, I have to be someone who can swallow my pride and need for justice and pray for bin Laden. I need to pray for leaders of other nations, no matter what their status.

It's God's job to take care of justice.

It's God who will deal with the sins of their world when they're long gone.

It's my job to pray.

It's my job to love.

IDENTIFYING WAYS TO LOVE YOUR ENEMIES

Have you ever been around someone who just got on your very last nerve?

Maybe she talks funny.

Maybe he talks too much.

Maybe she acts weird.

Or maybe he just bugs every square inch of your soul. That's the person I'm talking about.

It's easy to love people who compliment you. It's simple to fish for compliments and line your life up with people who agree with you.

It's godly to reach out to those who bother you. But it's a fruit-bearing disciple who can put aside her personal vendettas and reach across the feelings of hate to encourage someone she doesn't like.

Okay, fine. So, how do you do that? How do you love people who don't love you back, or may not want you to be involved in their lives at all?

Take a second and think about the kinds of people you like.

Think about the things people do for you that mean something in your life.

When someone brings you a gift, or writes you an encouraging note, or smiles at you, or maybe just says something kind when it's unexpected, it warms your heart. We all want to be loved. We all want to have people in our lives who are interested in us and notice the things we do well.

To love someone you don't like, you have to proactively seek out ways to encourage him. You have to meet her needs. You have to reach out like Jesus did for you.

Don't forget...before you accepted Jesus, you were an enemy of the cross. You weren't forgiven of your sin. And if God wasn't so loving, God probably wouldn't like you very much, either. Remember, we aren't trying to reproduce the world's way of thinking. We're not going to imitate revenge just because the world can justify our actions.

In order to be true loving disciples of Jesus, we have to love people.

Right now, sit down and identify two people in your life who you don't get along with. Target them. Make them the center of your day today and try to reach out and show them the love Jesus came to give you. I promise, if you can jump this hurdle, you're almost there.

HOW TO LIVE HUMBLY IN SPITE OF YOUR ENEMIES' SUCCESSES

One thing that ticks me off more than anything is watching someone who I dislike become successful.

I look up to heaven and say, "God, look at him. Look at what he did to me. He doesn't deserve to be rewarded for his actions. I mean, look at me."

And all of a sudden, God hits me right in my spiritual gut. "For by the grace given me I say to every one of you: Do not think of yourself more highly than you ought, but rather think of yourself with sober judgment, in accordance with the measure of faith God has given you" (Romans 12:3).

It's not about me. This life has nothing to do with who's successful in the world's eyes. God says to think of yourself with sober judgment, in accordance with the measure of faith God has given *you!*

I have no right to decide whether someone is successful or not. It's not my design. It's not in my ability. The only person I am responsible for is me.

My actions.

My attitude.

My willing spirit to choose to love those who don't deserve my love.

After all, that's exactly what Jesus did for me.

Take a meeting or two with your duplication partner and identify by name people you consider "enemies." Don't broadcast your list across the intercom at school; just keep it between you two. Then after you've identified those people, come up with a plan for how you're going to learn to love them.

Loving enemies isn't something that comes naturally. In fact, the opposite is true. We naturally want to lash out at enemies, not pray for them. We want to get revenge, not try to serve them. It's going to take a conscious choice, but in order to have the same spirit Jesus had with his enemies as they hung him on a cross to die, you've got to start forgiving and serving. Try it. You might be surprised how Jesus becomes more real to you today.

HOW DID WE GET HERE?

In the beginning, God created the heavens

and the earth.

—GENESIS 1:1

I walked into my freshman biology class at the largest Christian university in the world. There were two or three hundred students in a large lecture hall, and we waited for our professor to start us in on pre-med biology. Looking back, I don't know why in the world I was taking pre-med biology. I wasn't going to be a doctor; I went to school to be an actor. But, in true Andy Braner fashion, I registered for the hardest classes to prove to myself I could do it if I wanted.

I was looking forward to the class because I love cutting stuff up and figuring out how things work. Biology seemed to be the place where I could put my scalpel to the test while learning about the foundational pieces of life on earth.

The door opened, and to my surprise, a short, stocky man hobbled through the doorway. He carried several folders under his arm, and he had a killer beard. I looked at my buddy across the aisle and mouthed, "Sweet beard!" It was Facial Hair Friday after all, and the freshmen in my dorm were trying to grow out as much face hair as possible over the weekend. This guy was totally the winner!

He stepped up to the podium and started in first thing. "Okay, you know you're in biology. You know we're going to cover evolution. If you have any disagreements with evolution, just sit there and be quiet. I don't have the time or energy to explain myself every semester. Darwin was right. You came from a monkey. And if you want to get an A in this class, you'll figure out how to accept it."

What?! I'd never heard such hubris in all my life. Is that science? Declaring something fact without allowing room for discussion or discovery surely doesn't seem like a valid teaching method to me. I'm all for conviction, but I was paying a lot of money to learn how to learn, not to sit in a class and have some guy just blurt out the truth with no room for discourse.

"Okay, now that we've got that out of the way, let's start with the cell. Turn in your books to chapter 1..."

I could hardly listen the rest of the hour. The dissident in me wanted to fight, but the realist in me made me sit and just accept the facts the good doctor was spewing. I didn't know how to respond, and I certainly wanted a good grade. What to do?

DID GOD CREATE THE WORLD?

My parents took me to church every chance they had. I was in the nursery three weeks after I was born. So naturally, I've heard the creation story a million times. "God created the world." I know! Can we move on to something else? *Please?*

But later on, I was in a state of confusion about this whole creation thing. At school, my teachers gave hard-core facts, but at church, the teachers were a little more like, "Just take it by faith, because that's the way it happened."

I didn't really care, to be honest. *No one was there in the beginning, so why do we have to fight about it? Does it really matter? Surely not.*

I didn't care, that is, until I realized the consequences.

DO I NEED TO STUDY EVOLUTION?

The consequences of the evolutionary theory are many. It's not like you can just dismiss the theory and try to hide it under the umbrella of science. Think about it:

If humans came from monkeys, then how do you explain Adam and Eve? Where did they come from? Were they just the first ones to make the transformation from monkey to human?

Think about the process of creation. God created birds, and then God created land animals. The evolutionists say dinosaurs turned into birds, and that's why we don't have any dinosaurs on earth today.

What about Adam's age? The Bible says Adam died when he was 930 years old. Isn't that a little crazy to think a human can live to 930? Why didn't God say Adam died when he was a million years old? It would be just as crazy, wouldn't it? If Adam was formed on day six, and God rested on day seven, and the days were millions and millions of years long, then why was Adam so "young" when he died?

You see, it does matter what you believe about creation. It forces you to either view Genesis as a metaphor or disagree with the Darwinian theory of evolution.

There are so many theories and possibilities about the nature of creation. You don't have to look too far to find one, examine it, and try to discover if it's truly necessary for you to believe in.

I don't think the creation story is *the* hill God wants us to die on. It seems as though the spirit behind the story is, God created man. God is interested in the little details of creating all we see. The psalmist says, "The heavens declare the glory of God, and the firmament shows His handiwork" (Psalms 19:1, NKJV).

It's important for your spiritual walk to understand that God created all things. God's interested in all the beauty around you. In the details. God has the power to do it however God wanted to do it. God established science and biology before we even had the chance to call it those names.

HOW DOES SCIENCE RELATE TO THE BIBLE?

If you think about the beginning of time as a starting place for everything that comes after, it only makes sense that God—if God created the sun, the moon, and the stars—certainly created the scientific laws that govern how those pieces of creation operate. In other words:

God created physics.

God created chemistry.

God created astronomy, geology, and biology.

God made all those things work together to form the earth we know today.

Without God's foreknowledge and understanding, we would be a mass of cosmic circumstance. We would be floating aimlessly through the universe with no hope, no purpose, and no real foundation for the way we live.

You see, I don't have problems with the science of evolution; I have problems with the conclusions. If you take the evidence and explain it away as gradual processes forming all we see today, you remove any sort of supernatural intervention.

If evolution is true, then my only purpose in life is to propagate DNA that allows humanity to continue the process of evolving to the next state.

There's no reason to base my life on giving, helping the poor, loving the needy, or just reaching out to a friend. My purpose centers on whatever makes me feel good at the time.

In other words, a pure evolutionist will hold to the idea that we're all just creatures of random existence looking for whatever roles allow us to experience the most pleasure. And that seems a little odd to me. And selfish.

Take murder, for example. What if I believe it's okay to take someone else's life? If I'm a true Darwinian evolutionist, with no God guiding my morality, wouldn't murder be an acceptable behavior? Who's to say I'm wrong? It's just different human opinion and relative viewpoints. No one is correct; no one is incorrect.

You might say, "Well, the government says so." But what if I lived in a place where the government didn't make it illegal? Think of Nazi Germany. Was it right to kill six million Jews just because the government allowed it? Was it right for Saddam Hussein to carry out genocide because he was the head of the government? Of course not.

There has to be some sort of right in the world that governs decision-making. Otherwise we're just spinning on this rock in a gradual freefall until someone has the guts to blow us all away.

So, our views on science *do* matter. Your view of science as it relates to the Bible helps you discover all that God has for you in every arena. Take some time to research what you think. Ask your teacher hard questions about where you came from. Let's agree together to figure out how and why God created us. It's an important discussion that must not be discarded simply because we weren't there to watch it take place.

CHAPTER TWENTY-FOUR

WHY DO THEY SING SO MANY SONGS AT CHURCH?

Sing praises to the LORD, O you his saints,
and give thanks to his holy name. For his anger is but for a moment, and his favor is for
a lifetime. Weeping may tarry for the night,
but joy comes with the morning.

—PSALM 30:4-5 (ESV)

W hen you mention worship in the context of the church, everybody has a different idea about what it is. Some people believe worship is music played on a big pipe organ like in the churches of old while others believe a one-man, one-guitar acoustic set is what's pleasing to the God, even though both of them would call the other a heretic.

Worship is a funny thing. Some people like instruments, and others outlaw them. Some people worship in a contemporary style, while others stick to the old hymns.

Paul asked the Romans to "present your bodies as a living sacrifice, holy and acceptable to God, which is your spiritual worship" (Romans 12:1, ESV).

Jesus told the woman at the well, "God is spirit, and those who worship him must worship in spirit and truth" (John 4:24, ESV).

In the Old Testament, David wrote, "Oh sing to the LORD a new song; sing to the LORD, all the earth! Sing to the LORD, bless his name; tell of his salvation from day to day. Declare his glory among the nations, his marvelous works among all the peoples! For great is the LORD, and greatly to be praised; he is to be feared above all gods" (Psalm 96:1-4, ESV).

Singing is a form of worship. Truth is a form of worship. Even our bodies are supposed to be a form of worship. So how do we reconcile all the different parts of worship and boil them down to the one thing we have to do to worship God?

WHAT IS "WORSHIP" IN THE BIBLE?

Can you picture worship in the Old Testament? "There you shall go, and there you shall bring your burnt offerings and your sacrifices, your tithes and the contribution that you present, your vow offerings, your freewill offerings, and the firstborn of your herd and of your flock. And there you shall eat before the LORD your

God, and you shall rejoice, you and your households, in all that you undertake, in which the LORD your God has blessed you" (Deuteronomy 12:5-7, ESV).

Worship was a sacrifice. The Old Testament believers worshiped not by bowing down to carved images and idols, but by bringing sacrifices to the temple and rejoicing that God gave them a way to be free. God made a way to reconcile humanity with himself despite their sin, and thus they had a reason to be joyful.

Obviously there isn't a place these days to take sheep or doves, but there is a way you can sacrifice. And that's exactly what I think worship is all about. It's about a sacrifice.

The New Testament says, "Offer your bodies" (Romans 12:1). But that doesn't mean we should set up altars to God and lie on them and be killed. The sacrifice called for is totally giving God your time, your efforts, your focus, your hopes, your plans, and your dreams. Not easy!

The Bible says, "The one who offers thanksgiving as his sacrifice glorifies me; to one who orders his way rightly I will show the salvation of God!" (Psalm 50:23, ESV). So maybe worship isn't just sacrificing lambs and goats. And surely worship isn't just a song from your mouth. So what is worship, and how can you do it?

HOW CAN I WORSHIP IN MY CHURCH?

Think about the different ways you can worship in your church. If we're supposed to offer our bodies as holy living sacrifices, how can we do that in real time today?

One of the first ideas that comes to mind is teaching. Have you ever asked anyone at your church if you could teach? What would it look like for a high school or college student to go to church and run the kindergarten Sunday school class? What a *blast!*

You could be worshiping God by teaching the kindergartners some of the Bible stories you know so well. You could be worshiping by helping them understand that God loves them. You could be worshiping by showing them how to pray, or how to listen, or how to focus on God's love in their lives.

You don't have to be some great and mighty teacher to help out a children's Sunday school class. You just have to be willing, and you have to be diligent. Don't sign up for a class unless you have the full intention of making it there every Sunday. Worship isn't something you can just pick every now and then. Worship is constant.

Maybe you're not into doing a little kids' Sunday school, but maybe you'd like to play an instrument in the church music program. Maybe you can sing or play the guitar or the drums; you can worship God with music.

Maybe you're an actor, and you feel like you can communicate God's truth through performance. Go to the elders of your church and offer a performance on a Sunday morning, a Wednesday night, or some other meeting time.

The worst thing they can say is "No, thank you." You'll never be able to worship God until you step out of your comfortable sphere of influence and try something new.

WHAT ARE OTHER WAYS TO WORSHIP GOD?

What if you don't want to teach, you don't have any music skill to speak of, and you're just wondering what gifts you can use?

Maybe you're in a position to worship God just by giving God the various areas of your life. Maybe worship for you is giving up your dating life to a pure and holy lifestyle. Maybe worship for you is in your media life. You could worship God through your friendships. You could worship God through your family. You might even worship God by the attitude you have today, because that's the real bottom line.

See, worship isn't, at the end of things, a series of actions; it's an attitude.

It's thankfulness that comes from your heart.

It's recognition that God is in control of all things in the universe.

It's a submission to God's ultimate will and a denial of your own wants and desires.

Don't get me wrong—God isn't in the business of stealing your joy. But God does require a sacrifice up front.

Don't be deceived. Again...God isn't some genie in a bottle where you can just rub the side and get three wishes. God is sitting on the throne of the universe, and God's chief desire is to give you the desires of your heart. "Delight yourself in the LORD, and he will give you the desires of your heart" (Psalm 37:4).

God isn't interested in you walking around being smug all day. God isn't interested in being worshiped purely from a sense of duty. God wants to give you the desires of your heart as you delight yourself in knowing the extent of God's love for you.

Be creative. Find ways in your life to offer praise and thanksgiving and truly worship God in spirit and in truth.

DO I REALLY HAVE TO GIVE ALL MY MONEY TO GOD?

Every tithe of the land, whether of the seed

of the land or of the fruit of the trees, is the

Lord's; it is holy to the LORD.

—LEVITICUS 27:30 (ESV)

The Christian journey is full of different disciplines. Praying, fasting, studying your Bible, and learning how to listen to God are all parts of a spiritual formation process. Sometimes one of the hardest lessons to learn is the one about giving.

Giving my life, I totally understand. Giving my time, I'm all about that. But for whatever reason, we find giving our hard-earned cash something of a stretch. I don't know why money is such a big issue. Maybe it's because we've created a society consumed with buying stuff. Maybe it's a question or a feeling that the church doesn't handle the funds the right way. Who knows? But every time I pull out my wallet to give to the church, I have a secret little voice that says, *You know that money would go further if you gave it somewhere else.*

It's such a silly game going on in my head, because—let's be honest—do we really think God *needs* our money? Come on. Get serious. If God needed money, God wouldn't be God.

God owns everything anyway. Think about it. Have you ever seen someone taking a truckload of cash to their grave? We don't really "own" stuff. We don't really control anything. But somehow in this life, we feel a sense of ownership, and it's tough to give it up.

We're only caretakers of the things in this life for a short time. That's why I think life has very little to do with cash, and to be honest, the discipline of giving isn't a means for God to get more. I think if God needed more money, God would cease to be the Creator. God can do whatever God wants to do, and a bountiful harvest surplus of money isn't the way God tends to create things. God didn't need money to create the world at the beginning of time, right?

No, I think the concept of giving tithes and offerings to other people is centered on another lesson all together.

WHY DO I NEED TO GIVE IF GOD OWNS ALL THE MONEY ANYWAY?

What's the core of the American dream? Nice house. Nice car. One mate. Two and a half kids. White picket fence. Small dog barking in the front yard. It's that scene we always see on television, where we think if we only had that life—the one on TV—everything would work out for us.

The Bible speaks clearly about money. "Keep your life free from love of money, and be content with what you have, for he has said, 'I will never leave you nor forsake you'" (Hebrews 13:5, ESV).

The love of money clouds our decisions. It blinds us to the most important things in life.

Just ask people with a lot of money. Ask them if it's easier being rich or easier being poor. Sure, you don't want for anything if you have everything. But if you have everything, you have to take care of it. You have to guard it. You have to worry if your lifestyle will continue to be what it is right now.

Giving isn't a discipline for God; it's a discipline for you. It's a way to work your finances and remind yourself each week: *I don't own anything.*

It's a promise each time you write a check or drop cash in a bucket: *All this stuff doesn't mean anything, because I don't own it anyway.*

True, it takes money to run a ministry. True, the money you give isn't going to some pit labeled, "Here lies Andy's lesson on giving." We have to give responsibly. But we also have to give cheerfully. The Bible says, "Each one must give as he has made up his mind, not reluctantly or under compulsion, for God loves a cheerful giver. And God is able to make all grace abound to you, so that having all sufficiency in all things at all times, you may abound in every good work" (2 Corinthians 9:7-8, ESV).

God is interested in you giving because you want to give. If you pull out your checkbook and grumble about how much you give the church, then just don't. Don't give anything. Remember, God doesn't need your money. God wants to teach you a lesson—mainly, that God owns it all.

The good consequences are obviously the lives you help with additional resources. You'll help the pastor feed his family. You'll help the church grow its programs. Hopefully a church centered on missions will be giving money to support good things around the world.

Not only do we get to learn about God's sovereignty, we also get to see our lesson help other people around the globe. Isn't God a good God?

WHO DO I GIVE TO?

In my family, obviously we contribute to our local church, but we feel obligated to give other places, too.

I have a folder in my desk containing all the people who've ever asked for money from me. Missionaries, ministry organizations, even some mission-trip people will write in. Unfortunately, I can't help everybody, but when the time comes to give, I try to shell out as much as I can to help other people enjoy the blessing God's given me.

There's no "right" organization to give to, just like there isn't a "wrong" way to do it. Check out the people you give to. Make sure you know how they're going to use the money you've given, so you can be responsible. And you can also follow up.

There's nothing cooler than being able to see something built, someone fed, or someone's life changed because God allowed you to give a little resource away.

Have you ever asked yourself, "What would I do with the money if I won the lottery?" Well, that's a good way to see exactly what you would do with the money. Try it out. If your list includes a new car, a new wardrobe, or other "things" that are supposed to make you happy, then tithing is a great discipline for you to start working into your life.

It's a great way to test your heart and see where you are on your spiritual journey. Money grabs hold of us for some reason, and when we have stuff, it's interesting to see where our hearts are. Do you know who you serve today?

Jesus said, "No one can serve two masters, for either he will hate the one and love the other, or he will be devoted to the one and despise the other. You cannot serve God and money" (Matthew 6:24, ESV).

Where your treasure is, the Bible says, *there your heart is as well* (Luke 12:34). The things you value in life will point directly to where your heart is.

HOW MUCH SHOULD I GIVE?

For sure, there isn't a magic number of cash you should give. The widow gave two mites (Mark 12:42-44). Jesus told his disciples she gave more than everyone else who contributed. Because she gave out of little and gave all she had, it meant more to him than those who gave a lot out of abundance.

So I suppose giving is a matter for which you'll have to search the depths of your heart.

My wife and I tend to give out of necessity. We look for needs and try to meet them. You might find you'll give out of projects that speak to your soul. The bottom line isn't so important to God. Remember, *God owns it all anyway!* You can't "out-give" God. You're not going to impress God. Give out of the necessity to learn the lesson and be disciplined.

I'm positive you'll find the joy in giving as you continue to seek God in all areas of your life.

BAPTISM: WHERE DID *THAT* COME FROM?

Baptism, which corresponds to this, now
saves you, not as a removal of dirt from the
body but as an appeal to God for a good
conscience, through the resurrection of Jesus
Christ.

—1 PETER 3:21 (ESV)

I must admit, from an outsider's point of view, this is the strangest part of Christian living. Some churches baptize kids on a certain day to dedicate them to God. Others baptize people when they confess Jesus as their Savior. Either way, it seems kind of odd that in order to be a part of the body of Christ, most churches mandate some form of baptism.

Basically baptism has something to do with water. There are some churches where the leader sprinkles water on the head of the person being baptized, while others have a virtual swimming pool behind the pastor where they actually submerge the new believer.

Even looking at churches around the world, some baptize in rivers, lakes, or oceans, and I read recently of a prison story where the prisoner was baptized in his cell using the water spout provided for brushing his teeth.

I don't demean this practice, but it makes sense to ask the question: Why?

Why do we do this thing called baptism?

Is it necessary?

Why are there so many different styles of baptism, and why do different churches do it differently?

I certainly want to respect the traditions of various systems, because I don't think anyone has the corner on the market when it comes to baptism. But if we read the Scriptures and find out where, when, and how people were baptized, it might shed a little light on why we do this underwater sacrament.

GOT BAPTISM?

The Old Testament doesn't speak of baptism at all. The first time the Bible references baptism is when John the Baptist comes on the scene. The Bible says, "John appeared, baptizing in the wilderness and proclaiming a baptism of repentance for the forgiveness of sins" (Mark 1:4, ESV).

Luke also recounts this strange man in the wilderness. "And he went into all the region around the Jordan, proclaiming a baptism of repentance for the forgiveness of sins" (Luke 3:3, ESV).

So John was the first one to use baptism with water to represent a new life. A new beginning. It was like he was giving the people a moment in time to remember washing off the old sinful nature and making a commitment to live differently from that point forward.

I'm not so sure John intended baptism to mean immediate salvation, but it seems as though he coupled this water event with a time in life when all things would be different.

I know several Christians who choose not to be baptized, and it's not because they don't want to; it just seems as though baptism isn't as important to them because they believe Jesus. They follow Jesus. They try to read his Word and obey his commandments. It's their first priority. I know others who believe baptism is an important component of salvation.

WHAT IS IT, AND WHY DO SO MANY DENOMINATIONS DIFFER ABOUT IT?

John the Baptist seemed to be calling people to a public display of their spiritual need for change. He exhorted people to repent and be baptized. It was almost like he was calling people to step out of their normal routine and show the world their remorse for the way they were living and calling them to a new beginning.

I know of many churches that hold to the tenet that baptism is just a symbol of belief. But I also know of churches that believe baptism is essential for salvation (1 Peter 3:21).

What *do* we know about baptism? Jesus did it. He didn't come to earth and try to skirt this sacrament. He walked down to the river with John the Baptist and asked John to baptize him.

"But John tried to deter him, saying, 'I need to be baptized by you, and do you come to me?' Jesus replied, 'Let it be so now; it is proper for us to do this to fulfill all righteousness.' Then John consented" (Matthew 3:14-15).

I propose that whatever the reason for baptism, it can't hurt. Even if it's simply a statement to the world that shows people what you believe, then do it. It can't hurt anything, and an event like baptism just strengthens your confidence in your own faith journey.

Remember, if we're imitating Jesus, and Jesus was baptized, it only makes sense to walk down to the river and follow him.

WHAT DID JESUS MEAN WHEN HE COMMANDED US TO EAT HIS BODY AND DRINK HIS BLOOD?

(ALL ABOUT COMMUNION)

Jesus said to them, "I tell you the truth, unless you eat the flesh of the Son of Man and drink his blood, you have no life in you.

—JOHN 6:53

It must have been an incredible sight to watch Jesus preach. John 6 details a real-life meeting between Jesus, the disciples, and 5,000 witnesses.

Can you imagine? They sat on a hill, Jesus at the bottom, the disciples sitting at his feet listening to every word out of this miracle healer's mouth. He was already gaining quite a reputation for being a man who could perform miracles over nature, and he even claimed to be able to forgive their sins.

The Bible doesn't describe the message. We don't know if Jesus was preaching about following God or about a husband treating a wife with respect. What we do know is that he was setting the stage for something great!

The message was about to end, and Jesus leaned over to Philip and said, "Where shall we buy bread for these people to eat?" (John 6:5).

He knew what he was doing (verse 6). The Bible says he already had a plan. He was testing Philip to see what the disciples' response would be. I suppose you can infer that he was ready to really put their faith to the test.

Crowds of people were following, but did they really believe Jesus could perform a miracle this big—feeding 5,000 people? (Actually, in Jesus' time, 5,000 referred to the number of men only; there could have been double the amount if they counted women and children.)

Can you imagine Philip's face when Jesus asked him where to buy bread? To Philip, it probably seemed as if Jesus were commanding him to go and find the money, the restaurant, and the catering company to deliver the food; and surely the crowd was getting hungry.

I don't know if you've ever seen a crowd go into a feeding frenzy, but if they were anything like American crowds, Philip knew they were about to have a problem.

They didn't have the money to feed all those people. They didn't have the resources even if they had the money. There wasn't a place where 10,000 people could sit down and eat all at the same time. What was Philip to do?

You've probably read the story before. If not, check it out in John 6. Jesus took five loaves of bread and two fish and prayed to God to supply their need. The Bible records that the meal was so bountiful the disciples picked up the scraps and filled 12 baskets with the leftovers. It was a miracle over nature.

The next day, Jesus began to teach the disciples about bread that would keep you from going hungry (verses 32-59). He gave them a history lesson of the Old Testament Israelites in the desert and reminded them of God's provision in their hunger by miraculously placing manna in the desert every morning for them to eat.

Then he recalled the miracle just performed in front of their eyes, as if to say, "Hey, guys, if I can provide you with physical food, don't you think I can provide you with spiritual food?" He says in John 6:53, "I tell you the truth, unless you eat the flesh of the Son of Man and drink his blood; you have no life in you."

He was making a point. You have physical hunger, but you also have spiritual hunger. If I can feed your physical body, don't worry—I'll take care of your spiritual body as well.

The New Testament is full of wonderful analogies of bread and water as sustenance for our bodies, as well as Jesus' provision and their meaning in our spiritual lives. Jesus even ends his three-year earthly relationships with his disciples by conjuring up an analogy of bread and wine as it relates to his body and blood.

WHY DID JESUS BREAK BREAD WITH THE DISCIPLES BEFORE HE WENT TO DIE?

Just like baptism, the other sacrament you can find in almost every church in the world is communion. It's the time when they pull out the silver offering plates full of broken crackers and grape juice—or whatever format your church uses.

Growing up, my pastor always used to tell us about how we are to remember Jesus by eating his body, represented by the bread, and drinking his blood, represented by the grape juice. And although I think remembering Jesus' death on the cross is vitally important, I don't think it's just Jesus' death that's cause for this ceremony.

Jesus took his disciples into an upper room to eat the last supper.

> While they were eating, Jesus took bread,
>
> gave thanks and broke it, and gave it to his
>
> disciples, saying, "Take and eat; this is my

body." Then he took the cup, gave thanks
and offered it to them, saying, "Drink from it,
all of you. This is my blood of the covenant,
which is poured out for many for the
forgiveness of sins."

—MATTHEW 26:26-28

What if he wasn't trying to tell the disciples to re-member the event of the crucifixion merely for the event itself? What if Jesus was actually trying to com-municate that the spiritual sustenance was about to be poured out? He commanded the disciples to remem-ber—but remember what?

WHY DO WE "DO COMMUNION" TODAY?

I think communion is one of those things we need to take a look at and ask ourselves if it's necessary to do it like we've always done it.

Imagine for a minute you were about to give some-one the gift of eternal life, but you were going to have to face the most excruciating torture known to the world to this point in order to give it. If she accepted your gift, would you want her reflecting on the sacrifice, or the gift?

I think Jesus wanted us to use communion as a rallying cry, not as a memorial. He wanted us to remember his sacrifice, sure; but I think he smiles down on us when we approach his throne with a joyful attitude of thanksgiving.

Thanksgiving. Don't we have a holiday like that?

Isn't Thanksgiving the time when all our families gather around one common table of thanks? We make certain foods to remember the pilgrims and their voyage to America. We give thanks for all the blessings we've had during the year, and often those blessings include loud, funny stories. Sometimes they even help us recall embarrassing moments. We tell jokes. We have serious talks. We sit around and remember—remember for the sake of our family here in America.

I wonder if communion should be the Christian Thanksgiving feast. What if we all gathered around a table and took communion like we eat Thanksgiving dinner? We remember the good times, we recall the sacrifice, and we celebrate the fact that Jesus came to die so we could live. Wouldn't that be cool?

WHO CAN PARTICIPATE IN COMMUNION?

I suppose if you're going to reinvent communion, it begs the question, who can give thanks?

Who are those free from sin?

Who has received eternal life through Jesus?

Who is set free from their old sinner selves and reconciled to a righteous God?

Who has experienced God's grace?

Who has accepted God's forgiveness?

Who is living an abundant life because of Christ's death?

Who is making disciples?

Who is obeying Jesus' commands?

Who really loves Jesus?

I suppose there's your answer.

WHAT'S THE DEAL WITH *LEFT BEHIND?*

You heard me say, "I am going away and I
am coming back to you." If you loved me, you
would be glad that I am going to the Father,
for the Father is greater than I. I have told
you now before it happens, so that when it
does happen you will believe.

—JOHN 14:28-29

just got an e-mail from one of my students, and
I thought it was worth sharing:

> I'm stuck in Revelation. It's just really hard
> to relate to anything in that particular book
> of the Bible, and it's disappointing because
> reading Scripture every night used to be
> what helped me keep my relationship with

God so strong. But now, when I could really use the inspiration in my spiritual life, I can't ever find anything that makes much sense. So basically, the point of all my rambling is that I was wondering if maybe you could give me any advice. I don't know whether there's something else I should be trying to do to help rebuild my relationship with God, or maybe I'm just not looking closely enough at Revelation.

Let's be honest here. We've all tried to tackle Revelation from a layperson's point of view. Inductively, Revelation makes no sense. You can't find answers to all the symbols in Revelation without some sort of outside help—and even scholarship on the subject is inconclusive. If you don't know the particulars of Hebrew culture meeting Greek culture, you're in trouble. Unless you've studied it extensively—or lived there at that particular time period—Revelation is confusing.

The book of Revelation is called apocalyptic literature. It's similar to Daniel in the Old Testament. Basically it's a message sent back to someone in code describing some form of the end of the world or impending prophecy.

Everybody wants to know about the end of the world, the beast coming out of the ocean, and the infamous 666 code. But the reality is, all those people trying to explain it—they're simply making their best educated guesses at this point in history.

For centuries Christians have tried to explain Revelation. Nero was supposed to be the Antichrist in the mid-first century, and many scholars say his Aramaic name adds up to the 666 code found in Revelation. If that's the case, Revelation is a historical book rather than a prophetic book. Now that would throw a wrench in the cog of mainstream evangelical theory!

Hitler is a more recent figure identified as the Antichrist. From the first century to the 21st century, we simply don't know when, we don't know how, and we don't know why the things in Revelation seem go down the way they do.

Brilliant scholars are still arguing over the time of the rapture, the length of the tribulation, and the literal meaning behind the millennium. (Don't read too much into this; I'm not advocating we rip Revelation out of the back of the Scriptures. The early church leaders obviously included Revelation for a reason, and we need to spend time learning why they wanted us to keep such a book. We simply can't excuse our unknowing to ignorance or lazy attitudes.)

It's important for you to know what's in Revelation. In fact, a special blessing is promised to those who read the book and attempt to understand it (Revelation 1:3). But for all of you who think you have the end of the world pinned down to the hour, please *stop*!

Stop scaring people.

Stop creating mindless zealots.

The fact of the matter is, no one knows when Jesus is coming back. Jesus told the disciples in a discourse at the end of Matthew, "Therefore keep watch, because you do not know the day or the hour" (25:13). In other words, every day should be like tomorrow is the last. Every hour should be treated as if Jesus will suddenly appear. We spend entirely too much time trying to equate Babylon to Iraq, the Antichrist to the secretary general of the United Nations, or the horsemen to supernatural plagues.

Jesus warned the disciples to be ready for his return but not to get too crazy because they didn't know the hour. Don't you think we should heed his advice?

SO, WHEN IS JESUS COMING BACK?

For the Lord himself will come down from
heaven, with a loud command, with the voice
of the archangel and with the trumpet call
of God, and the dead in Christ will rise first.
After that, we who are still alive and are left
will be caught up together with them in the
clouds to meet the Lord in the air. And so we
will be with the Lord forever.

—1 THESSALONIANS 4:16-17

This book is entirely too short to disclose all the theories of revelation, but I'll try to help you with a few. The two words you need to know when studying Revelation are *tribulation* and *rapture*.

TRIBULATION

The tribulation is supposed to be a period of time on earth when everything that can go bad will. "Concerning the coming of our Lord Jesus Christ and our being gathered to him, we ask you, brothers, not to become easily unsettled or alarmed by some prophecy, report or letter supposed to have come from us, saying that the day of the Lord has already come. Don't let anyone deceive you in any way, for that day will not come until the rebellion occurs and the man of lawlessness is revealed, the man doomed to destruction. He will oppose and will exalt himself over everything that is called God or is worshiped, so that he sets himself up in God's temple, proclaiming himself to be God" (2 Thessalonians 2:1-4).

Most modern evangelical scholars believe the tribulation is a seven-year time period when the world is going to be filled with lawlessness and destruction. But remember, it's merely an educated inductive guess. We're not totally sure how it will go down, but that's the current theory.

CHAPTER TWENTY-EIGHT

RAPTURE

The rapture is thought to first have been discussed in 1 Thessalonians when Paul speaks of being caught up in the clouds with Jesus (1 Thessalonians 4:16-17). A little interesting part of history is that the rapture wasn't talked about anywhere in Christianity until 1830, when a man named John Derby tried to reinvent the way we read the Bible. A man named Cyrus Scofield took Derby's platform and wrote the Scofield Study Bible, which is the most popular Bible sold today.

I'm not saying the rapture won't happen, but it's important to take into consideration that the *Left Behind* story has roots only 170 years old in a religion that spans thousands of years.

The point is, we just don't know how or when it's going to go down.

Some people believe Christians will be taken up to Jesus before the tribulation begins—pre-tribulation rapture.

Others believe there's a decisive event in the middle of the tribulation when Christians will be taken out of the earth—mid-tribulation rapture.

And most early church fathers believed Christians would endure the tribulation and then wait on Jesus' return—post-tribulation rapture.

For your sake and mine, I hope it's before the world begins to erupt, but there are so many holes in every theory, it remains to be seen, just as Jesus told his disciples. And it doesn't change the bottom line.

And that bottom line is that God is in control. His plan is going to unfold one way or another. Just relax a bit and try to focus on what's going on around you.

There are 153 million orphans in the world. What are you doing to help that problem? Maybe instead of focusing our resources on trying to discover the time and hour of Jesus' return, we should take a little bit of time trying to undo problems we're facing *now*.

HOW IS HE COMING?

Jesus is coming back. He told us he would, and he told us he's coming back like a thief in the night (1 Thessalonians 5:2).

Just like a thief arrives at a home undetected, Jesus is going to return when we least expect it.

We know he's going to come back like a flash of lightning (Luke 17:24). Just like the lightning flashes from the east to the west in a big thunderstorm, Jesus is going to come. He's coming quickly. He's coming in a flash. He's coming in a visible way.

He came the first time in a manger, relatively unknown to the majority of the world. But the second time around, there will be no mistake. Jesus is coming in a decisive way. How do I know?

He said so. The Bible is clear on this point.

IS JESUS' RETURN *THAT* IMPORTANT?

It's one of the most important parts of our faith. Jesus' return is the hope of all believers. His eventual victory over the forces of evil and the power over the earth is the way the world will be fully reconciled to God.

As you look around the planet and ask yourself how a good God could let all this stuff go on—things like starvation, ethnic cleansing, and the rising numbers of orphans in every country—remember that someday, God will make all things new.

Most people missed his first arrival, but if the Bible is to be taken seriously, they won't miss it the second time.

It's important you know the difference in all the Revelation theories so you can make up your mind. You need to allow the Spirit to lead you to truth, just like Jesus promised. Gos isn't a God of confusion. God doesn't want us to walk around ignorant. God is interested in Revelation, but be careful not to let any one person dictate the theory of Revelation to you. Know your history.

You live in the most educated time in all the earth. You have access to information no person in history has ever had. Just because a new novel, a new movie, or a new charismatic leader claims to have the truth nailed for this book, be careful. Jesus said no man knows the hour, and the book of Revelation is full of symbolism.

In order to understand this book, it's going to take a lot of study and a lot of open-mindedness. Ask your pastor what your church believes. Ask other ministers from other denominations what they believe. And then let the Holy Spirit lead you to the truth.

The answer is out there. It's just going to take a little brain work.

WHAT IF I'M ASKED A QUESTION, AND I DON'T KNOW THE ANSWER?

(THEN YOU'VE ARRIVED)

—ANDY BRANER

The best adventures in life hold mysteries around every corner. The most beautiful scenery in the world is unexpected.

A sunset over a mountain range is unplanned.

A rainbow spanning the horizon doesn't bow to any calendar of events.

The waves crashing against a craggy cliff are predictable, but the one that explodes with foam right in front of your face is a total surprise.

Your journey in your spiritual life will be filled with unanswered questions, and surprises are only moments away. That's what makes this adventure so fun. It's not possible for you to know every answer about every theological question. There's no way. You don't have enough life experience to be able to correlate every Bible verse to some kind of application right now. And that's *totally okay.*

Education is filled with questions, and when those are answered, a new crop of inquiries emerges. They're unplanned, they're not accounted for, and most times they lie right across your path waiting for you to stumble upon them. There's no shame in admitting to someone that you don't know the answer. In fact, when I'm teaching, much of the time, I just have to say, "I don't know, but let's find out. *Together.*"

I love questions without obvious answers. They give me purpose as a teacher. As a discipler, those questions push me to understand God's grand mysteries in my own life. I don't know how God deals with predestination. I get confused when I think of Jesus living a life as totally God and totally man. It's tough. There are complex issues in the Bible that require a great deal of thinking, exploration, and experience. Don't be scared.

Remember, no question you have is going to knock God off the throne of the universe. Just because you can't answer in no way nullifies thousands of years of Christianity.

BEING CONFIDENT

Be confident that God is still God. Rest assured that the answers are out there.

Be aggressive as you try to find out what the Bible says about modern issues.

Remember Isaiah's experience with God? Check this out.

> In the year that King Uzziah died, I saw the
> Lord seated on a throne, high and exalted,
> and the train of his robe filled the temple.
> Above him were seraphs, each with six wings:
> With two wings they covered their faces, with
> two they covered their feet, and with two
> they were flying. And they were calling to one
> another:
>
> "Holy, holy, holy is the LORD Almighty; the
> whole earth is full of his glory." At the sound
> of their voices the doorposts and thresholds
> shook and the temple was filled with smoke.
>
> —ISAIAH 6:1-4

The experience God allowed Isaiah to have in the presence of his throne room was almost indescribable.

Can you imagine having a real encounter with the living God in the midst of angels singing? What if you stood before God, and the smoke started filling the room, and the thunderous chants of angelic beings thumped so loud you could feel it in your bones? Would you be scared? Would you be intimidated?

I think Isaiah probably was terrified. It must have been totally weird to stand before God like that. The most important consequence of this meeting was that Isaiah's view of God was seared in his mind for a lifetime.

That's exactly how our view of God should be. If you haven't met God in a similar way, and I mean a real life-altering way, take a break. Take a journey to seek God's face. God promises that as we seek him, he will reveal himself to us, and when you're standing confident before the throne of God, "I don't know" becomes an answer of humility rather than a confession of ignorance.

BEING EDUCATED

"I don't know" is a good answer to start with, but don't relax and start using it as a crutch to get through hard passages. The ability of Americans to think through tough issues has become progressively weaker over time, and we must be knowledgeable people.

If you don't understand something, great! Go figure it out. Find other people who have written about the subject. At no other time in human history have Christians been so educated. We have information coming in and out of our lives at a constant pace. You can Google, turn on the television, rent a documentary, reference a commentary, or read one of the thousand Christian books released this month. You have the tools—use them.

We have too many ignorant Christians in the world afraid of discovering ideas that may disturb their current thinking. Don't be afraid. Let down your preconceived notions, and allow God to take you on a journey to know him.

God is not a traditional God. God's not one who abides by what we humans believe. Just look at the men and women of the Bible. They didn't see a God just walk past sickness and hunger. They watched as Jesus supernaturally healed their friends. And Jesus is waiting for you to know him today. He longs for you to discover his wisdom and power through spiritual wisdom and understanding.

Don't let "I don't know" just flow from your lips without a passionate pursuit for truth. Our faith demands it.

BEING HUMBLE

Jesus never set up a kingdom here on earth—not one with thrones and armies anyway. He was born in a stable. He took on fishermen, tax collectors, and normal working guys as his disciples.

He came from the majesty of heaven with all the angels awaiting orders and gave himself over to the confines of frail humanity.

If Jesus did that for you, rest confident knowing that you can humble yourself before the people you disciple. You can invite people from all walks of life into this adventure called duplication, and as you seek to imitate, believe, and become a follower of Jesus, they'll follow someone who is real. Be real. Be humble. Be educated.

Now go! Be encouraged. Duplicate yourself as you try to imitate, believe, and become a follower of Jesus. Go out and make some disciples.

Love This! contains real-life stories of people like you who've found ways to love their neighbors. It will challenge you to make a difference in your world by loving people who are often ignored or unloved—the homeless, the addicted, the elderly, those of different races, even your enemies—and show you tangible ways you can demonstrate that love.

Many people think teenagers aren't capable of much. But Zach Hunter is proving those people wrong. He's only fifteen, but he's working to end slavery in the world—and he's making changes that affect millions of people. Find out how Zach is making a difference and how you can make changes in the things that you see wrong with our world.

Be the Change
Your Guide to Freeing Slaves and Changing the World
Zach Hunter
RETAIL $9.99
ISBN 0-310-27756-6

Visit www.invertbooks.com or your local bookstore.